This Devotional Belongs to:

Contact us via email:hello@chatterboxtherapists.comor by phone (256) 299-5877

Visit: www.chatterboxtherapists.com

Please leave a review on Amazon or whatever bookstore you order your book from.
Your input and feedback matter to us.

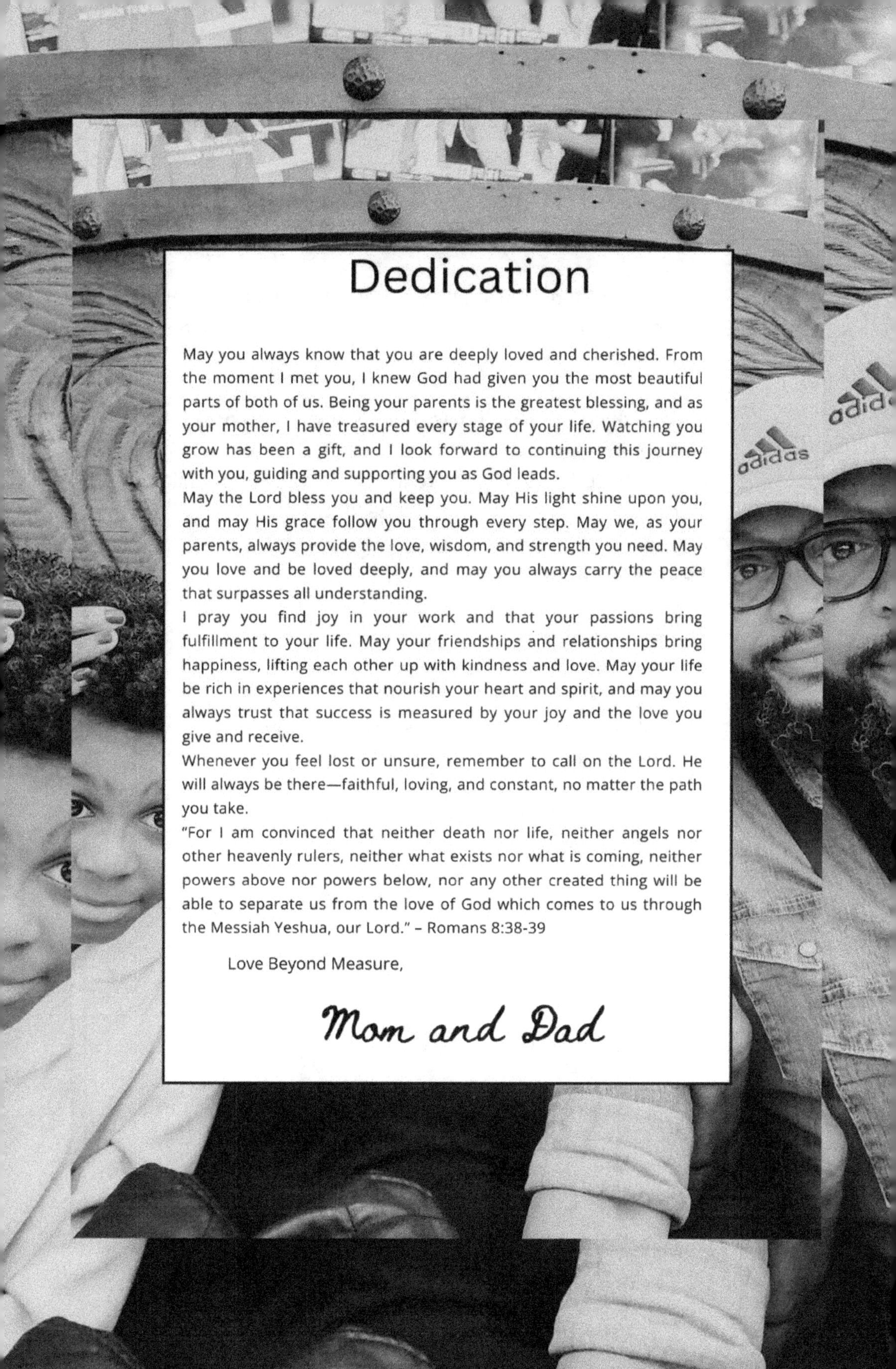

Dedication

May you always know that you are deeply loved and cherished. From the moment I met you, I knew God had given you the most beautiful parts of both of us. Being your parents is the greatest blessing, and as your mother, I have treasured every stage of your life. Watching you grow has been a gift, and I look forward to continuing this journey with you, guiding and supporting you as God leads.

May the Lord bless you and keep you. May His light shine upon you, and may His grace follow you through every step. May we, as your parents, always provide the love, wisdom, and strength you need. May you love and be loved deeply, and may you always carry the peace that surpasses all understanding.

I pray you find joy in your work and that your passions bring fulfillment to your life. May your friendships and relationships bring happiness, lifting each other up with kindness and love. May your life be rich in experiences that nourish your heart and spirit, and may you always trust that success is measured by your joy and the love you give and receive.

Whenever you feel lost or unsure, remember to call on the Lord. He will always be there—faithful, loving, and constant, no matter the path you take.

"For I am convinced that neither death nor life, neither angels nor other heavenly rulers, neither what exists nor what is coming, neither powers above nor powers below, nor any other created thing will be able to separate us from the love of God which comes to us through the Messiah Yeshua, our Lord." – Romans 8:38-39

Love Beyond Measure,

Mom and Dad

Hey You!

Whoever gifted you this Biblical Blueprints 90-Day Devotional: Preteen by Chatterbox Therapists cares about you deeply.

It's one thing to say we care, but it's another to pray for someone – and the greatest gift of all is showing you how to build a meaningful relationship with God while learning to care for your mental health.

You are worth it.

You deserve to be:

- Seen for who you truly are
- Heard when you have something to say
- Understood even when words are hard to find
- Encouraged to follow your dreams
- Supported during tough times
- Celebrated for your uniqueness
- Surrounded by love and kindness

Always remember how valuable you are – and how much you are loved.

Navigating the pre-teen years is an exciting yet challenging journey. To support your child through this phase, we've created a Biblical Blueprint, for Preteens with 90 devotions specifically designed to foster meaningful discussions, strengthen family bonds, and guide kids as they learn to make thoughtful, biblically based decisions.

What's Inside:

90 Days of Devotions: Each daily devotional offers an age-appropriate scenario, Bible verse, and prayer that create opportunities for open conversations and reflection. These devotions are designed to be read with parents, guardians, or mentors, making space for shared experiences, learning, and bonding.

Culturally Inclusive Stories: The scenarios are crafted to reflect diverse experiences, ensuring all children can relate to and learn from the stories.

Complex Decision-Making Opportunities: Life is rarely black and white, and our scenarios reflect that. There can be more than one "right" answer, allowing kids to explore different choices, understand their consequences, and recognize the complexity of real-life decisions.

Empathy and Understanding: Kids are encouraged to think about the feelings and perspectives of others, helping them develop compassion and empathy. They will learn to understand someone's reasoning without always agreeing with their actions—a valuable skill for emotional intelligence.

Biblical Guidance: Each scenario is followed by a thought- provoking question, a carefully chosen Bible verse, and a simple prayer, helping kids connect their everyday choices with biblical teachings.

Topics Covered Include:

Fear, Anxiety, and Peer Pressure: Helping kids learn to cope with worries and make strong choices in difficult situations.

Friendships, Boundaries, and Integrity: Guiding children to build healthy relationships and stand up for what they believe is right.

Family Challenges: Addressing complex topics like mental illness, incarcerated parents, blended families, and feeling neglected.

Big Emotions and Self-Control: Teaching kids how to navigate big feelings, practice patience, and make wise decisions.

Practical Life Skills: Lessons on routines, chores, money management, planning their day, and setting goals.

Empathy and Kindness: Encouraging kids to see the world from another person's perspective and make choices that reflect compassion and understanding.

Difficult Conversations: Topics include dealing with issues like bullying, abuse, hygiene, self-harm, and mental health, handled in an age-appropriate and sensitive manner.

Why Biblical Blueprints Devotional Stands Out:

Fosters Family Bonding: Each devotion is designed to be read together, sparking discussions that help strengthen the bond between children and their caregivers.

Encourages Spiritual Growth: Rooted in biblical teachings, these devotions help kids apply faith-based principles to their daily lives and understand the importance of relying on God's guidance.

Prepares Kids for Real-Life Situations: By exploring various scenarios, this devotional equips children with the tools to handle challenging situations confidently and compassionately.

Supports Emotional Intelligence: The thought-provoking questions help kids reflect on their own feelings, recognize their values, and develop empathy towards others.

This 90-day devotional is an excellent resource for parents, teachers, and church leaders who want to help children navigate life's complexities with a strong moral compass. It's designed to *open meaningful conversations, build character, and guide kids toward making positive, faith-driven decisions.*

Give your child a powerful start to their spiritual journey with a devotional that nurtures their heart, mind, and soul—one day at a time.

mean·ing

ˈmēniNG/ • noun /

1. what is meant by a word, text, concept, or action.

Definitions of Words and Terms

A

- Absent Parents: A parent who is not regularly present in a child's life, which can be due to different reasons like work, living far away, or other circumstances.
- Abuse: When someone hurts another person's body, feelings, or makes them feel unsafe. Abuse can be physical, emotional, or even happen online.
- Alopecia: A condition that causes someone to lose their hair. It can happen to anyone and isn't something you can catch from someone else.
- Anxiety: Feeling very worried or nervous about something, sometimes so much that it's hard to think about anything else.
- Asking for Permission: When you check with an adult or someone in charge before doing something, to make sure it's okay.

B

- Being Abusive to Their Pet: Hurting or mistreating an animal on purpose. Pets need kindness and care, just like people.
- Being the Middle Child: A child who has older and younger siblings. Sometimes they might feel stuck in the middle or overlooked.
- Being the Oldest Child: The first child born in a family, who often has more responsibilities, like helping take care of younger siblings.
- Being the Youngest Child: The last child born in a family, who might feel like they are treated as the baby of the family.
- Big Feelings: Strong emotions like anger, sadness, excitement, or fear that can feel overwhelming.
- Blended Families: A family where parents have children from previous relationships and may also have new children together.

- Bullying: When someone repeatedly hurts, teases, or makes fun of another person on purpose to make them feel bad.

C

- Cool Kids: A group of people who are popular and others want to hang out with, even if they sometimes make poor choices or are mean.
- Copying Homework: When you take someone else's work and pretend it's your own. It's dishonest and doesn't help you learn.

D

- Debt: Money that someone owes and needs to pay back. It happens when you borrow money and promise to return it later.
- Different Types of Families: Families can look different—some have one parent, two parents, step-parents, or even grandparents raising kids.
- Doing Chores: Tasks like cleaning, washing dishes, or helping with groceries that kids can do to help their family.

E

- Embarrassed: Feeling shy, silly, or uncomfortable about something you did or something that happened to you.
- Eviction: When someone is forced to leave their home because they can't pay rent or have broken the rules of where they live.

F

- Foster Care: A system where children live with a different family when their parents cannot take care of them.
- Friend Comes to School with Bruises: When a friend has injuries that look like they were hurt. It's important to tell an adult if you're worried about them.

G

- Gossiping: Talking about someone behind their back, often saying things that are unkind or untrue. Grooming: When an adult builds trust with a child to take advantage of them. It can be dangerous and is a type of abuse. Grief and Loss: The deep sadness you feel when you lose someone you care about, like a friend or family member.

H

- Hygiene: Keeping yourself clean and healthy, like brushing your teeth, washing your hands, and taking showers.
- Homeless Student: A child who doesn't have a permanent place to live and might stay in different places like shelters or with friends.

I

- Inappropriate Touching: When someone touches your body in a way that makes you feel uncomfortable or is not allowed. It's important to tell a trusted adult if this happens. Integrity: Doing the right thing even when no one is watching.

J

- Judging Others: Making assumptions or negative comments about people without really knowing them.

K

- Keeping Secrets for Friends: Deciding whether a secret is safe to keep or if it's something that should be told to an adult because it could be dangerous.

L

- Lying: Saying something that isn't true on purpose. It can hurt others and break trust.

M

- Money Problems: When there isn't enough money to pay for things that a family needs.
- Monthly Mishap: When a girl starts her menstrual cycle, also known as a period. It can be unexpected and sometimes embarrassing.

N

- Negative Thoughts: When you keep thinking bad or unhelpful things about yourself or situations.
- Neglect: When a child doesn't get the care and attention they need from their parents or caregivers.

O

- Online Safety: Being careful about what you do on the internet and making sure not to share personal information with strangers.

P

- Peer Pressure: When friends or people around you try to get you to do something you might not want to do.
- Planning for Your Day: Making a list of things you need to do during the day to help you stay organized.

R

- Red Flags: Signs that something might be wrong or unsafe.
- Routines: Doing certain things at the same time every day, like brushing your teeth before bed.

S

- Self-Care: Taking time to do things that make you feel good and healthy, like exercising or reading a book.
- Self-Harm: When someone hurts themselves on purpose because they are feeling very sad or upset. It's important to talk to an adult if you or someone you know is feeling this way.
- Suicidal Thoughts: When someone feels so hopeless and sad that they think about ending their life. It's very serious and important to get help right away.

T

- Team Player: Someone who works well with others and helps their group or team succeed.
- Trustworthy: A person who is honest, keeps their promises, and can be relied on.

V

- Vaping: Inhaling vapor from an electronic cigarette. It's unhealthy and can be dangerous, especially for kids.

W

- What Are Bills? Monthly payments that adults need to make for things like rent, electricity, and water.
- What is Debt? When someone owes money and needs to pay it back.

Y

- You Had One Job: When someone makes a mistake doing something that seemed simple or straightforward.

How to Use This Devotional

Welcome! This guide will help you get the most out of your devotional journey.

1. Take Your Time
   There's no rush! Reflect deeply on each day's message. It's okay to spend more time on a devotional if you need it.

2. Do at Least One Devotional Per Day
   Aim to complete one devotional daily. Consistency helps build a strong spiritual and mental wellness routine.

3. Discuss or Reflect Alone
   You can choose to complete each devotional on your own or share your thoughts with loved ones. Both approaches are meaningful—find what feels right for you.

4. No Wrong Answers
   Be honest with yourself. There are no wrong answers, only your personal reflections and insights. Trust your journey and learn from each experience.

5. Enjoy the Process!
   This devotional is a tool for growth, reflection, and healing. Embrace it, have fun, and let it bring you closer to peace and understanding.

Take it one day at a time and let God guide your steps!

MY MISSION STATEMENT

DESIGN PROCESS REPORT

What's a Mission Statement? It's a simple way to write down what's important to you, what kind of person you want to be, and how you can make good choices every day!			
Step 1: What Do You Care About? **Write down three things you care about:**			
1. Positive and healthy relationship with my family. 2. Fairness 3. God's favor			
Step 2: What Kind of Person Do You Want to Be? **Circle the words that describe you or how you want to be:**			
Kind	Brave	Fair	Courage
Honest	Helpful	Gratitude	Boundaries
Respectful	Patient	Integrity	Empathy
Step 3: What Are Your Big Goals? What do you want to do in life? It could be helping others, being a great friend, or doing something fun and creative! Write down 2-3 goals:			
1. I want to help my family when they need me. 2. Being fair is important to me, everyone should be treated fairly. 3. I want my life to reflect a positive relationship with God.			
Step 4: Your Mission Statement			
Example Mission Statement: "I want to be a kind and honest person who helps my family when they need me. I will try my best to be fair and trust God every day."			

MY MISSION STATEMENT

What's a Mission Statement?

It's a simple way to write down what's important to you, what kind of person you want to be, and how you can make good choices every day!

Step 1: What Do You Care About?
Write down three things you care about:

1.

2.

3.

Step 2: What Kind of Person Do You Want to Be?
Circle the words that describe you or how you want to be:

Kind	Brave	Fair	Courage
Honest	Helpful	Gratitude	Boundaries
Respectful	Patient	Integrity	Empathy

Step 3: What Are Your Big Goals?

What do you want to do in life? It could be helping others, being a great friend, or doing something fun and creative! Write down 2-3 goals:

1.

2.

3.

Step 4: Your Mission Statement

"I want to be a ______________________________(kind, brave, etc.) person who ______________________________ (helps others, makes good choices, etc.). I will ______________________________ (work hard, stay positive, trust God, etc.) to make the world a better place."

my mission statement

TOPICS

90 Topics

Topic 1: Fear
Topic 2: Anxiety
Topic 3: Peer Pressure
Topic 4: Integrity
Topic 5: Red Flags and Funny Feelings
Topic 6: Setting Boundaries
Topic 7: Grooming
Topic 8: Who Can I Trust?
Topic 9: Self-Harm
Topic 10: Keeping Secrets for Friends
Topic 11: Suicidal Thoughts
Topic 12: Bullying
Topic 13: Hygiene
Topic 14: Money
Topic 15: Different Types of Families
Topic 16: A Student in Foster Care
Topic 17: An Unhoused Student
Topic 18: The Importance of Routines
Topic 19: Planning for Your Day
Topic 20: Planning for Your Week
Topic 21: Being a Team Player
Topic 22: Doing Chores
Topic 23: Playing Sports
Topic 24: Money Problems
Topic 25: Being Embarrassed
Topic 26: Big Feelings
Topic 27: Grief and Loss
Topic 28: Trending
Topic 29: Stealing
Topic 30: Hygiene II
Topic 31: Abuse
Topic 32: Secrets and Trust
Topic 33: Suicidal Thoughts
Topic 34: Bullying
Topic 35: Different Types of Families
Topic 36: A Student with Alopecia
Topic 37: A Displaced Student
Topic 38: You Had One Job
Topic 39: Friend Comes to School with Bruises
Topic 40: Unfair Treatment by the SSO
Topic 41: The Math's Not Mathing
Topic 42: How Would They Know?
Topic 43: Crushed
Topic 44: Closed Mouths Don't Get Fed
Topic 45: Feeling Lost
Topic 46: Rocket Science
Topic 47: Negative Thoughts
Topic 48: Soggy Sleepover
Topic 49: Trying New Foods
Topic 50: Asking for Permission
Topic 51: When They Tell You No
Topic 52: Changing Your Mind
Topic 53: Feeling Embarrassed
Topic 54: Money Issues
Topic 55: Grief and Loss
Topic 56: Finders Keepers
Topic 57: Parents with Mental Illness
Topic 58: Incarcerated Parents
Topic 59: Absent Parents
Topic 60: Blended Families
Topic 61: Feeling Neglected
Topic 62: Mom's Favorite Child
Topic 63: Losing a Sibling
Topic 64: Being the Youngest Child
Topic 65: Being the Middle Child
Topic 66: Being the Oldest Child
Topic 67: Monthly Mishap
Topic 68: Weird and Embarrassing Changes
Topic 69: A Friend is Being Abusive to Their Pet
Topic 70: Inappropriate Touching
Topic 71: Visiting a Friend's Dirty Home
Topic 72: A Parent's Addiction
Topic 73: Vaping
Topic 74: Running Away
Topic 75: Understanding Why Your Parents Are Tired
Topic 76: What Are Bills?
Topic 77: What is Debt?
Topic 78: How Can I Be Prepared Financially?
Topic 79: Watching Bad Videos Online
Topic 80: Gossiping
Topic 81: Staying Home Alone
Topic 82: The Cool Kids
Topic 83: Sneaky Crush
Topic 84: A Teachable Moment
Topic 85: Positive Punishments?
Topic 86: Learning How to Prioritize
Topic 87: Self-Care
Topic 88: Asking for Forgiveness
Topic 89: Lying
Topic 90: Good Choices and Self-Control

Topic 1: Fear

Jenny has to give a presentation in front of the class, but she feels really scared. She's worried that everyone will laugh at her if she makes a mistake.

What would you do?

- ☐ Ask the teacher if you can skip the presentation.
- ☐ Take deep breaths and remind yourself that you can do this.
- ☐ Ask a friend to help you practice.

Have you ever felt scared to do something? Describe it below.

Think about how Jenny felt when she was nervous about presenting in front of the class. What do you think was going through her mind?

What does the Bible say? "Don't be afraid, for I am with you. Don't be discouraged, for I am your God. I will strengthen you and help you. I will hold you up with my victorious right hand." – Isaiah 41:10

Prayer: "Dear God, sometimes I feel scared to do new things. Please help me to remember that You are always with me and that I don't have to be afraid. Give me the courage to face my fears with strength. Amen."

Topic 2: Anxiety

Caleb's parents are going on a trip for a few days, and he's nervous something bad will happen while they're away. He can't stop worrying about it.

What would you do?

- ☐ Stay up all night worrying about what might happen.
- ☐ Talk to your parents about how you're feeling.
- ☐ Pray and ask God to help you feel safe.

Have you ever felt worried like Caleb? Describe it below.

Think about how Caleb might be feeling, constantly worrying about his parents. How do you think this worry affects his day?

What does the Bible say?
"Give all your worries and cares to God, for he cares about you." – 1 Peter 5:7

Prayer:
"Dear God, sometimes I feel worried about things like Caleb does. Please help me to trust that You are watching over my family and keeping them safe. Help me to feel calm and know that You are in control. Amen."

breathe...

inhale

slowly and deeply through the nose

four to six counts

exhale

slowly through the mouth

four to six counts

Topic 3: Peer Pressure

Maya's friends are pressuring her to skip school with them to go to the mall. Maya doesn't feel right about it, but she's afraid they'll stop being her friends if she says no.

What would you do?

- ☐ Go with them so you don't feel left out.
- ☐ Tell them that you don't want to get in trouble and suggest something else to do.
- ☐ Talk to a teacher or adult for advice.

Have you ever felt like Maya, where friends wanted you to do something you didn't feel comfortable with? What happened?

Imagine how she must feel wanting to fit in but also knowing it's wrong.

What does the Bible say?
"Don't follow the crowd in doing wrong." – Exodus 23:2

Prayer:

"Dear God, sometimes it's hard to stand up for what's right when my friends want me to do something I know isn't good. Help me be strong and make the right choice, even when it's hard. Amen."

Topic 4: Integrity

Jake finds a $20 bill on the ground at school. No one saw him pick it up, and he's tempted to keep it, but he knows it doesn't belong to him.

What would you do?

- ☐ Keep the money and buy something you want.
- ☐ Turn the money into the office and see if someone claims it.
- ☐ Ask a friend what they would do.

Have you ever found something valuable that wasn't yours? What did you do? What would you do differently?

Think about how Jake might be feeling when he has the chance to do the right or wrong thing.

What does the Bible say?
"The godly walk with integrity; blessed are their children who follow them." – Proverbs 20:7

Prayer:
"Dear God, help me to always choose what is right, even when no one is watching. Help me be honest and do what honors You. Amen."

WE DEMONSTRATE:

LEADERSHIP

COURAGE

EMPATHY

FAITH

KINDNESS

AUTHENTICITY

INTEGRITY

Topic 5: Red Flags and Funny Feelings

Sophie has a neighbor who's always trying to get her to come over to his house, even though her parents don't know him very well. It makes her feel uncomfortable, but she doesn't want to be rude.

What would you do?

- ☐ Go to the neighbor's house just to be polite.
- ☐ Tell your parents about the situation and how you feel.
- ☐ Avoid the neighbor but keep it a secret.

Have you ever had a strange feeling around someone? What happened?

Think about how Sophie might feel in this situation and what that funny feeling might mean.

What does the Bible say?
"The prudent see danger and take refuge, but the simple keep going and pay the penalty." – Proverbs 22:3

Prayer:

"Dear God, help me to trust my feelings when something doesn't seem right. Help me to talk to a parent or trusted adult when I feel uncomfortable. Keep me safe and aware. Amen."

Topic 6: Setting Boundaries

Liam's friend Mark keeps making fun of him in front of other people, and Liam feels hurt. He doesn't want to lose his friend, but he also doesn't want to keep being teased. Mark acts differently when they are alone, which is confusing to Liam.

What would you do if your friend made fun of you?

- ☐ Keep quiet and let your friend continue teasing you.
- ☐ Tell your friend how you feel and ask them to stop.
- ☐ Stop hanging out with your friend altogether.

Have you ever had a friend who hurt your feelings? What happened?

Think about how Liam might feel, wanting to stand up for himself but not wanting to lose his friend.

What does the Bible say?
"Do to others whatever you would like them to do to you." – Matthew 7:12

Prayer:
"Dear God, help me to set good boundaries with my friends and treat others the way I want to be treated. Give me the courage to speak up when someone is hurting me. Amen."

SET BOUNDARIES

Protect Your Well Being with Healthy Boundaries

Understand Your Limits

Get to know your personal limits in various aspects of life, such as time, energy and emotions. Knowing your limits helps you maintain balance and prevent burnout.

Learn to Say No

Don't hesitate to say no when something exceeds your capacity. Saying no is your right to protect your time and energy. Prioritize your own needs without feeling guilty.

Prioritize Self Care

Make self care a top priority. Make time for activities that calm and restore energy, such as exercise, meditation, or reading. Self-care helps you stay healthy and happy.

Topic 7: Grooming

Emma's older cousin Bobby keeps giving her gifts and asking her to keep secrets from her parents. She feels special but also unsure about keeping secrets. She's been hiding the gifts from her parents. She likes getting gifts, but she feels conflicted, because this feels so wrong.

- ☐ Keep the gifts and keep it a secret.
- ☐ Tell your parents or another adult about what's happening.
- ☐ Try to handle it on your own without getting anyone involved.

What do you think their motivation would be for having you keep this secret?

Describe how Emma feels, wanting to keep the gifts, but feeling weird about it.

What does the Bible say?
"Have nothing to do with the fruitless deeds of darkness, but rather expose them." – Ephesians 5:11

Prayer:
"Dear God, please help me to recognize when something isn't right, even if it looks good on the outside. Help me to talk to a parent or adult when I feel unsure. Amen."

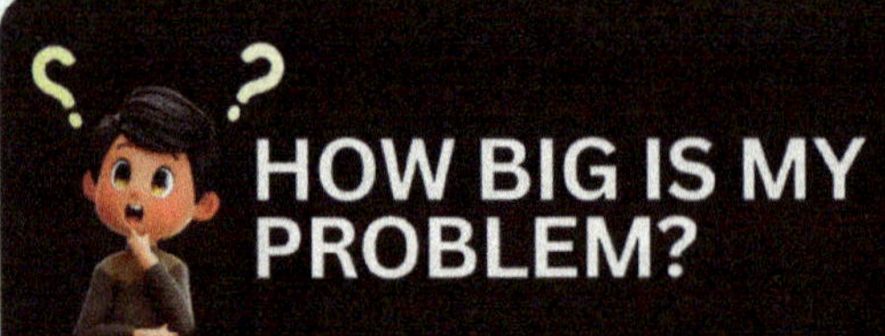

HOW BIG IS MY PROBLEM?

Students need to build emotional resilience and problem-solving skills. This chart will help students put their issues into perspective and identify the scale of their problem.

	Causes	What can be done?
5 Emergency	• Earthquake • Fire • Danger to yourself/others	I CAN cry, scream, yell for help, feel worried or scared
4 Huge	• Someone touching you without permission • Fighting • You are badly hurt	I CAN tell a trusted adult, walk away, call for help, go to the nurse
3 Large	• Someone pushes/hits you • You don't feel well • Someone is making fun of you • Someone says a bad word • Conflict with a friend	I CAN tell a teacher or a trusted adult, feel frustrated or disappointed
2 Medium	• Lost something • Someone cheated in a game • Not understanding my work • Can't use the gadget	I CAN take a break and calm down, talk about or write down my feelings, feel frustrated or irritated
1 Small	• Someone said something mean • Disagreements • Someone is bothering you • Not being called by the teacher	I CAN take deep breaths, use my words to solve a problem
0 Glitch	• Not being first in line • Someone takes your pencil • Getting a problem wrong	I CAN take a deep breath and continue on, feel disappointed

WWW.CHATTERBOXTHERAPISTS.COM

Topic 8: Who Can I Trust?

Zach isn't sure who to talk to when he's feeling upset. His friends sometimes make fun of him when he talks about his feelings, and he doesn't know who to trust. He has been wanting to share what he's going through, but he's nervous.

What would you do?

- ☐ Keep your feelings to yourself and deal with it alone.
- ☐ Find a trusted adult or friend who listens well.
- ☐ Ignore your feelings and try to be tough.

Who do you trust with your feelings? Why do you trust them?

Imagine how Zach might feel being afraid to open up to people around him.

What does the Bible say?

"Whoever walks in integrity walks securely, but whoever takes crooked paths will be found out." – Proverbs 10:9

Prayer:

"Dear God, help me to find people I can trust who will listen and care about my feelings. Help me to know who will support me when I need help. Amen."

WHO CAN I TRUST?

PEOPLE THAT I CAN CALL WHEN I NEED TO TALK

name **number**

name **number**

name **number**

name **number**

name **number**

My Address:

Topic 9: Self-Harm

Kayla's best friend, Carmen, has been scratching her arms when she gets upset. She hides the scratches with long sleeve shirts. Kayla is worried but doesn't know how to help.

What would you do?

☐ Tell Carmen to stop, but not mention it to anyone else.
☐ Encourage Carmen to talk to a trusted adult and offer to go with her.
☐ Ignore it because it's not your problem.

Why do you think people do things to harm themselves?

Describe how Kayla might be feeling as she tries to help her friend.

What does the Bible say?
"The Lord is close to the brokenhearted and saves those who are crushed in spirit." – Psalm 34:18

Prayer:
"Dear God, please help me understand when I or someone I know is hurting. Help me to find strength and talk to someone who can help. Guide me to show love and kindness to those in pain. Amen."

The Importance of Mental Health Awareness

01

Mental health awareness involves understanding and recognizing the importance of mental well-being and the impact of mental health on overall quality of life.

02

Mental health awareness helps reduce stigma, promotes empathy, and encourages open conversations about mental health concerns.

03

Increased mental health awareness leads to early recognition and intervention of mental health issues, improving outcomes and preventing further distress.

04

Mental health awareness helps reduce stigma, promotes empathy, and encourages open conversations about mental health concerns.

Topic 10: Keeping Secrets for Friends

Slone's friend, Chase, tells her that he's been sneaking out at night to meet up with older kids. He tells Slone not to tell anyone or they won't be friends anymore. Slone is worried about Chase, because she knows that the older kids do things that could get him in trouble.

What would you do?

- ☐ Keep the secret because you don't want to lose your friend.
- ☐ Talk to a trusted adult about it, even if Chase gets mad.
- ☐ Try to convince Chase to stop sneaking out but keep it to yourself.

Have you ever felt like you had to keep a secret that made you uncomfortable?

Describe how Slone might feel when her friend asks her to keep a dangerous secret.

What does the Bible say?
"Faithful are the wounds of a friend; profuse are the kisses of an enemy." – Proverbs 27:6

Prayer:
"Dear God, help me to know when it's okay to keep a secret and when it's important to tell someone who can help. Give me courage to do the right thing, even if it's hard. Amen."

NATIONAL Suicide Prevention

THERE IS HELP, THERE IS HOPE.

If you're facing challenges things that are too hard to deal with alone, please know there are people who care about YOU!

PEOPLE WHO CAN HELP.

- → TALK TO A TRUSTED ADULT
- → CALL 988 FROM A CELL PHONE
- → HTTPS://CHAT.988LIFELINE.ORG:
- → TEXT 988 IF YOU PREFER TEXTING
- → CALL 911 IN THE CASE OF AN EMERGENCY

WWW.CHATTERBOXTHERAPISTS.COM

WE NEED YOU HERE

"One step at a time. You'll get there."

Topic 12: Bullying

Annette is being teased every day on TikTok and SnapChat. They make fun of her posts and they've started bullying her little sister. She doesn't want to go to school anymore because her classmates make mean comments under her posts as well. She asked to sit next to you at lunch. Your friends are rejecting her and telling her that she can't sit there.

What would you do?

- ☐ Stay silent and hope the bullying stops on its own.
- ☐ Stand up for Annette and tell a teacher.
- ☐ Ignore the situation because it's not your problem.

Have you ever seen someone being bullied or been bullied yourself?

Describe how Annette must feel being treated this way every day.

What does the Bible say?

"Do not be overcome by evil, but overcome evil with good." – Romans 12:21

Prayer:

"Dear God, help me to show kindness to others and stand up for people who are being hurt. Give me courage to speak up when I see something wrong. Amen."

BREAKING THE CYCLE:

ANTI-BULLYING & STRESS RELIEF FOR TEENS

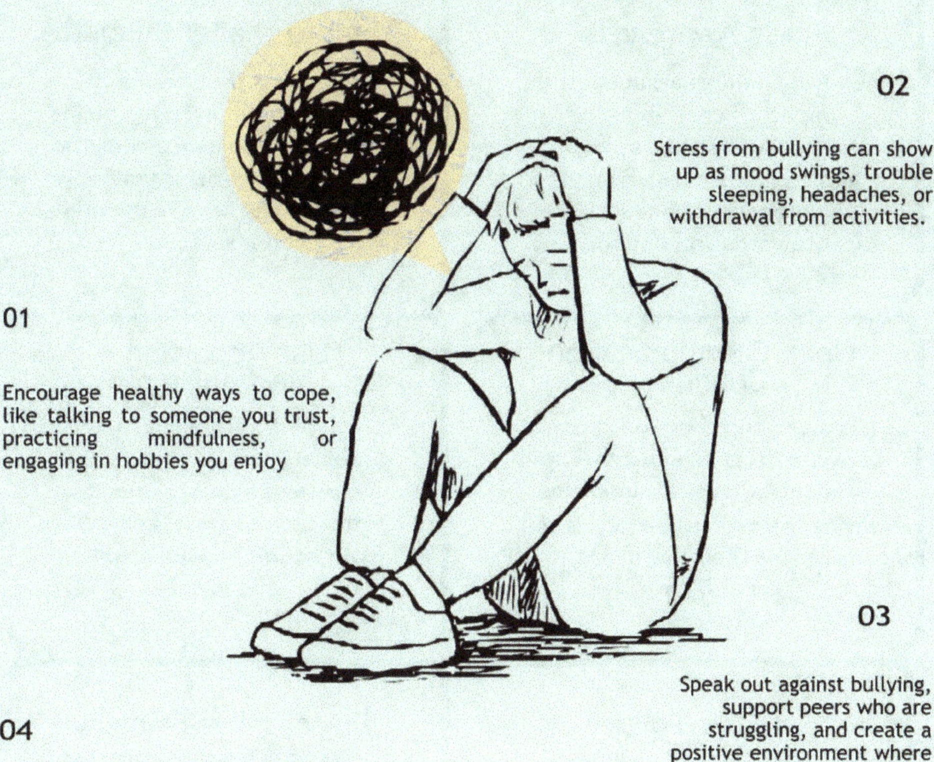

01

Encourage healthy ways to cope, like talking to someone you trust, practicing mindfulness, or engaging in hobbies you enjoy

02

Stress from bullying can show up as mood swings, trouble sleeping, headaches, or withdrawal from activities.

03

Speak out against bullying, support peers who are struggling, and create a positive environment where everyone feels safe.

04

bullying isn't just hurtful words; it's a major source of stress for teens. This stress can lead to anxiety, depression, and even physical health problems.

Together, we can reduce stress and end bullying. Take a stand for your well-being.

WWW.CHATTERBOXTHERAPISTS.COM

How to Stop Cyber-Bullying?

Raise Awareness

Educate individuals about the impact of cyber-bullying through workshops, seminars, and social media campaigns. Awareness is the first step towards prevention.

Promote Digital Etiquette

Encourage the practice of respectful communication online. Teach the importance of digital etiquette, emphasizing that words shared online have real-world consequences.

Open Communication Channels

Foster open communication between parents, educators, and students. Create a supportive environment where individuals feel comfortable reporting incidents of cyber-bullying.

Use Reporting Mechanisms

Implement reporting mechanisms on social media platforms and websites. Empower users to report incidents easily, and ensure swift action is taken against offenders.

Set Clear Policies

Establish and enforce clear anti-cyber-bullying policies in schools and workplaces. Ensure consequences for perpetrators and support for victims.

Teach Online Empathy

Incorporate empathy education into school curricular. Help students understand the feelings of others and the potential harm caused by cyber-bullying.

WWW.CHATTERBOXTHERAPISTS.COM

Topic 13: Hygiene

Jackson notices that Bruce has been smelling bad lately and some kids are starting to make fun of him. Bruce doesn't seem to realize it's a problem. He's a nice guy and he doesn't bother anyone.

What would you do?

- ☐ Tell Bruce in private so he can take care of it.
- ☐ Ignore it and hope someone else talks to him.
- ☐ Tease Bruce like the other kids do.

Have you ever had a time when you didn't realize something embarrassing about yourself? How did you feel?

What would you like someone to say to you if your hygiene was off?

What does the Bible say?

"Whatever you do, work at it with all your heart, as working for the Lord." – Colossians 3:23

Prayer:

"Dear God, help me take care of myself in ways that show respect for my body and help others who might need a little reminder. Help me to speak kindly to those who need it. Amen."

Topic 14: Money

Kingston has been saving his allowance for a new video game. His friend Caden wants to borrow money to buy snacks, but Kingston isn't sure he'll pay it back. Caden is pressuring Kingston to let him have the money every day.

What would you do?

- ☐ Lend Caden the money and hope he pays it back.
- ☐ Keep your savings and explain to Caden why you can't lend him the money.
- ☐ Give Caden half the money and ask him to repay the rest.

What would you do if your friend pressured you into giving them something that you saved for yourself?

Describe how Kingston might feel trying to be a good friend but also wanting to save for his video game.

What does the Bible say?

"The rich rule over the poor, and the borrower is a slave to the lender." – Proverbs 22:7

Prayer:

"Dear God, help me to be wise with the money I have and learn how to help others in a way that's fair and responsible. Teach me to make good choices about saving and sharing. Amen."

Topic 15: Different Types of Families

Antonio is new to the school, and when the teacher asks everyone to talk about their family, Antonio says he lives with his two dads. Some kids make fun of him because his family looks different from theirs.

What would you do?

- ☐ Make fun of Antonio because his family is different.
- ☐ Stand up for Antonio and tell the kids to stop.
- ☐ Talk to Antonio after class to make sure he's okay.

What makes your family unique?

Describe how Antonio might feel being teased for something out of his control.

What does the Bible say?

"Love one another. As I have loved you, so you must love one another." – John 13:34

Prayer:

"Dear God, help me to love and accept all families, even if they look different from mine. Help me be kind to people who might feel alone. Amen."

Topic 16: A Student in Foster Care

Carmen overhears her new classmate, Joy, talking about moving into another foster home. Carmen doesn't know much about foster care and wonders how she can be a good friend to her.

What would you do?

- ☐ Ignore it because you don't understand foster care.
- ☐ Ask Joy if she needs help and listen to her story.
- ☐ Ask a teacher how you can learn more about foster care to support your classmates.

What do you know about foster care?

Describe how Joy might feel moving around a lot and trying to make new friends.

What does the Bible say?

"Defend the cause of the weak and the fatherless; uphold the rights of the poor and oppressed." – Psalm 82:3

Prayer:

"Dear God, help me be a friend to those who are in foster care or don't have a permanent home. Help me show them Your love and make them feel accepted. Amen."

Topic 17: An Unhoused Student

Noah notices that Brad has been wearing the same clothes for a while and seems quieter than usual. He finds out from hearing a teacher say that Brad's family is living in a shelter right now.

What would you do?

- ☐ Tell your friends and make fun of Brad behind his back.
- ☐ Ask Brad what he needs and talk to your parents about helping him out.
- ☐ Ignore the situation because it's uncomfortable to think about.

Have you ever known someone who was going through a hard time like Brad?

Describe how hard it must be for him to come to school while living in a shelter.

What does the Bible say?

"Blessed are those who have regard for the weak; the Lord delivers them in times of trouble." – Psalm 41:1

Prayer:

"Dear God, please help me see those in need and show kindness to them. Help me be a friend to people who are struggling and teach me to be generous. Amen."

Topic 18: The Importance of Routines

Caden is always rushing in the mornings because he forgets to prepare the night before. He gets to school late, misses breakfast, and feels tired in class.

What would you do?

- ☐ Help Caden plan a morning routine so he has enough time.
- ☐ Tell Caden to wake up earlier, even though it's hard for him.
- ☐ Ignore the situation because it's not your problem.

Is being on time important? Why or why not?

Write how Caden feels every morning rushing and starting the day stressed.

What does the Bible say?

"Let all things be done decently and in order." – 1 Corinthians 14:40

Prayer:

"Dear God, help me to create routines that make my days better. Help me prepare so I can have a good start each day and use my time wisely. Amen."

Topic 19: Planning for Your Day

Annette has a busy day ahead with homework, a soccer game, watching her younger siblings and chores. She's not sure how to manage her time and feels overwhelmed. She wants to hang out with her friends but she doesn't have time. She has been looking sad lately.

What would you do?

- ☐ Help Annette write down a plan for the day to make time for friends.
- ☐ Tell Annette to pick one thing to focus on and forget the rest.
- ☐ Ask Annette if she could talk to her mom about her schedule.

Have you ever had a day where you didn't know how to fit everything in? What did you do?

Describe how Annette feels with so many things to do.

What does the Bible say?

"Commit to the Lord whatever you do, and he will establish your plans." – Proverbs 16:3

Prayer:

"Dear God, help me to plan my day well, so I can get things done without feeling overwhelmed. Teach me to ask for help when I need it. Amen."

SCHEDULE

Monday

Tuesday

Wednesday

Thursday

NOTE

Friday

WWW.CHATTERBOXTHERAPISTS.COM

Topic 20: Planning for Your Week

Noah has a project due on Friday, but he keeps putting it off. Now it's Thursday night, and he's stressed out about finishing it on time. He thought he had more time to finish his project and he knows that his dad will take his phone if he misses another assignment. You have been telling Noah to focus for the past three weeks. You finished your project early and you are proud of yourself. Now, Noah asked you to help him complete his assignment, but you have plans to hang out with your friends.

What would you do?

- ☐ Help Noah finish his assignment and miss hanging out with your other friends.
- ☐ Tell Noah to work through the night to get it done.
- ☐ Let Noah figure it out on his own.

How do you manage completing your homework on time?

Describe how Noah might feel scrambling to complete his project. Do you think he regrets procrastinating?

What does the Bible say?
"The plans of the diligent lead to profit as surely as haste leads to poverty." – Proverbs 21:5

Prayer:

"Dear God, help me plan my week in a way that leaves time for all the important things. Teach me to be diligent so I don't feel rushed. Amen.

A MINDFUL WEEK

S	Something you can accomplish next week.
M	Say something kind to yourself.
T	Write down something you are grateful for.
W	Find a moment to take five deep breaths.
TH	Do a quiet and calming activity you enjoy.
F	Celebrate something you achieved this week.
S	Observe what you see, hear, and smell outside.

A MINDFUL WEEK

S

W

TH

F

S

Topic 21: Being a Team Player

Kayla is on a group project with Slone and Jackson. She feels like she's doing all the work, while they play around and don't take it seriously.

What would you do?

- ☐ Talk to Slone and Jackson to remind them they are a team.
- ☐ Tell the teacher, so they get in trouble.
- ☐ Let them do what they want and just finish the project by yourself.

Have you ever had to work with people who weren't pulling their weight? What did you do?

Describe how Kayla might feel doing all the work on her own.

What does the Bible say?

"Two are better than one, because they have a good return for their labor." – Ecclesiastes 4:9

Prayer:

"Dear God, help me work well with others and be a good team player. Teach me to communicate and share responsibilities with the people around me. Amen."

Topic 22: Doing Chores

Chase's parents asked him to clean his room and take out the trash. But Chase keeps getting distracted by video games and forgets to finish his chores. You're on the phone with Chase and you are in the middle of a video game. You hear his parents ask him to get off of the game, but he ignores them.

What would you do?

- ☐ Remind Chase that chores are his responsibility, and it's important to help out at home.
- ☐ Tell Chase he can finish the chores later after more video games.
- ☐ Ignore it and let Chase get in trouble when his parents find out.

How do you feel about doing chores?

Describe how your parents feel when you do your chores properly.

What does the Bible say?

"Whatever you do, work at it with all your heart, as working for the Lord, not for human masters." – Colossians 3:23

Prayer:

"Dear God, help me to do my chores without complaining and with a positive attitude. Let me see the value in helping my family. Amen."

Daily Cleaning Tasks for Kids

Learning the importance of cleaning the house must be used in daily activities so that it will be habitual for a long time. Here are some chores you can perform as daily tasks.

Bedroom

Make beds after they wake up every time. And remember to tell them to organize their toys where they should.

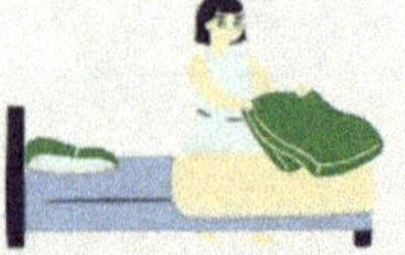

Kitchen

Encourage children to help with household chores by assigning them tasks such as washing dishes and placing them on the organizing rack, and helping to set the table during dinner.

Make a List of Your Daily Tasks

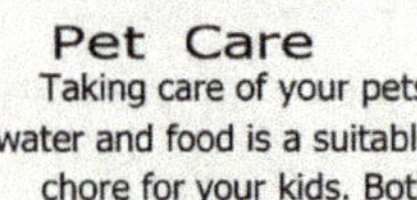

Pet Care

Taking care of your pets' water and food is a suitable chore for your kids. Both cleaning and loving other creatures are the lessons to be learned here.

Laundry

Teaching them how to sort the colors of clothes is essential before washing them. Then let the kids help you dry the clothes on the hanger.

Bathroom

You can tell them to clean the counter and mirror using the microfiber cloth. Also refill the toilet paper.

Living area

Since they usually play with their toys and dolls there, tell them to collect their toys from under the couch or carpet that they never check.

Topic 23: Playing Sports

Carter loves basketball, but sometimes he gets frustrated when his team doesn't play well. He wants to win, but sometimes he thinks about quitting when it's tough. He practices daily and he does his best in every game. He asks you your opinion about his situation.

What would you do?

- ☐ Encourage Carter to keep playing and focus on having fun and improving his skills.
- ☐ Tell Carter he should quit if he's not winning.
- ☐ Let Carter be frustrated and wait to see what he decides.

How do you feel about quitting?

Describe how Carter might feel when things don't go as planned.

What does the Bible say?
"Let us not become weary in doing good, for at the proper time we will reap a harvest if we do not give up." – Galatians 6:9

Prayer:

"Dear God, help me to keep going even when things are tough. Teach me to enjoy playing and to be a good sport, no matter the outcome. Amen.

Topic 24: Money Problems

Antonio's parents have been stressed about money lately. They told him they might not be able to afford a birthday party this year, and Antonio feels sad and embarrassed. Antonio had already told his closest friends about his party. You're the first one that he talks to about not having a party this year.

What would you do?

- ☐ Tell Antonio that birthdays are about spending time with people who love him, not just the party.
- ☐ Tell Antonio that he shouldn't talk about a party that he's not having.
- ☐ Avoid talking about it because it's uncomfortable.

Describe the last time you were disappointed.

Describe how Antonio feels missing out on something important.

Describe how Antonio's parents feel about having to cancel Antonio's party.

What does the Bible say?

"Keep your lives free from the love of money and be content with what you have." – Hebrews 13:5

Prayer: "Dear God, help me to be thankful for the things I have and the people who care about me. Teach me to find joy in the simple things. Amen."

Topic 25: Embarrassing

Carmen tripped and spilled her lunch in front of everyone in the cafeteria. She's embarrassed and doesn't want to go back to school the next day. She called you after school and told you that she plans on skipping school to avoid being bullied.

What would you do?

- ☐ Encourage Carmen to laugh it off and go back to school with confidence.
- ☐ Tease Carmen because it's funny, and everyone else is laughing.
- ☐ Avoid talking to Carmen because it's an embarrassing situation.

How important are other people's opinions? Why?

Describe how Carmen might feel after she spilled her lunch in front of everyone in the cafeteria.

What does the Bible say?

"For I am convinced that neither death nor life, neither angels nor demons, neither the present nor the future...will be able to separate us from the love of God." – Romans 8:38-39

Prayer:

"Dear God, when I feel embarrassed, help me remember that Your love is more important than what others think. Help me move past my mistakes with courage. Amen.

ALL ABOUT ME

HELLO

My name is

I am from

FUN FACTS

FAVORITE COLORS

FAVORITE FOODS

FAVORITE QUOTE

Topic 26: Big Feelings

Corey has been feeling really angry lately. Sometimes he doesn't know why, but he feels like he might explode. He's afraid to talk to anyone about it. You notice that he's been quiet lately and you're concerned about him.

What would you do?

- ☐ Encourage Corey to talk to someone he trusts about his feelings.
- ☐ Tell Corey it's normal to feel angry and let it pass.
- ☐ Let Corey keep his feelings inside because they're too difficult to talk about.

Have you ever felt strong feelings and didn't know what to do with them? Describe those feelings below.

Describe how Corey might feel holding in his anger.

What does the Bible say?

"In your anger, do not sin. Do not let the sun go down while you are still angry." – Ephesians 4:26

Prayer:

"Dear God, help me understand my feelings and give me the courage to talk to someone when I'm feeling upset. Teach me how to manage my anger in a healthy way. Amen."

Topic 27: Grief and Loss

Sherrie's grandmother passed away, and she's feeling sad and lost. She doesn't know how to talk about her feelings and feels like no one understands.

What would you do?

☐ Sit with Sherrie and listen to her talk about her grandmother.
☐ Tell Sherrie to try and get over it because it's part of life.
☐ Give Kayla space and avoid her because your grandma is still alive.

Have you ever lost someone you loved? How did it make you feel?

Describe how Kayla feels losing someone important in her life.

What does the Bible say?

"Blessed are those who mourn, for they will be comforted." – Matthew 5:4

Prayer:

"Dear God, please comfort me when I'm sad and help me to remember the good times with the people I love. Amen."

Topic 28: Trending

Jackson's neighbor Samuel always has the newest trends, the best clothes, the newest phone, the most expensive shoes and he doesn't even have to do chores or have good grades to get it. In fact, he often yells at his parents and storms out of his house after slamming the front door. Jackson noticed Samuel watching Jackson play football with his friends. He was tempted to ask him to come play with them, but before he could say anything, Samuel yelled, "What are you looking at loser!" Jackson and his friends were surprised at his reaction. Jackson paused, and he thought about the consequences of interacting with Samuel, if he is too nice, Samuel may want to hang out and he isn't a very nice person. If he is rude to Samuel, he could create an enemy, and they have to see each other because they live across from each other. He Is confused about what he should do.

What should Jackson do?

- ☐ Yell back at Samuel, "I'm looking at someone lonely who doesn't have any friends!"
- ☐ Ignore Samuel and continue playing football with your friends.
- ☐ Invite Samuel over to play football with them.

Do you have negative friends? If you have a friend like this, how do you usually feel after interacting with them?

What does the Bible say?

"Keep company with the wise and you will become wise. If you make friends with stupid people, you will be ruined."– Proverbs 13:20

Prayer: "Dear God, help me to choose friends that are kind and cool in their own ways. Amen."

GROUNDING
TECHNIQUE

A calming technique that connects you with the present by exploring the five senses.

5 things you can **SEE**

4 things you can **TOUCH**

3 things you can **HEAR**

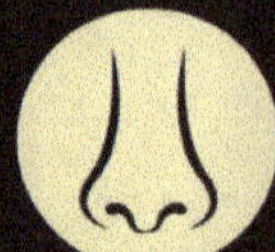

2 things you can **SMELL**

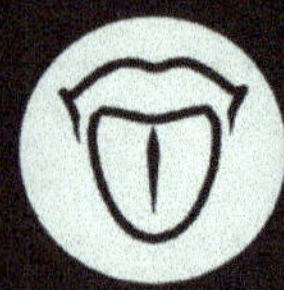

1 thing you can **TASTE**

Topic 29: Stealing

Jamie took some candy from the school store without paying for it. Now, he's afraid of getting caught and feels guilty.

What would you do?

☐ Tell Jamie to return the candy and apologize.
☐ Encourage Jamie to keep it and share some with you.
☐ Ignore it because it's just a small thing.

Have you ever had someone steal something from you? How did you feel?

Describe how Jamie might feel now that he's done something wrong.

What does the Bible say?

"You shall not steal." – Exodus 20:15

Prayer:

"Dear God, help me to be honest in everything I do. Teach me to respect other people's things and always do the right thing. Amen."

Topic 30: Hygiene II

Mark's friends noticed that he's been coming to school without brushing his teeth or showering. They don't want to hurt his feelings but are worried about him. He appears to be ashamed of his hygiene and you feel like something is wrong. You find out that he is staying with his dad this weekend and he doesn't have anything for his hygiene over his dad's house.

What would you do?

- ☐ Gently let Mark know that the front office may have some hygienic products for him.
- ☐ Bring Mark a bag of products and give it to him in private.
- ☐ Ignore it because it's not your place to say anything.

How do you feel about hygiene? Is it important? Why or why not?

How do you think Mark feels about his situation?

What does the Bible say?

"Suppose a brother or a sister is without clothes and daily food. If one of you says to them, 'Go in peace; keep warm and well fed,' but does nothing about their physical needs, what good is it?" -James 2:15-16

Prayer: "Dear God, help me to be kind to others and to be a blessing by how I treat them, even if I can't provide anything to help them. Amen."

Topic 31: Abuse

Annette has been feeling uncomfortable around her uncle lately. He says things that make her feel weird and sometimes touches her in ways that don't feel right. She's scared to tell anyone because she doesn't want to cause trouble. The family admires her uncle, and she doesn't want to make anyone angry.

What would you do?

- ☐ Encourage Annette to talk to a trusted adult about how she feels.
- ☐ Tell Annette to keep quiet so she doesn't make things worse.
- ☐ Ignore it and hope Annette figures it out on her own.

Have you ever felt uncomfortable but didn't know how to tell someone?

Describe how Annette might feel, confused and scared.

What does the Bible say?

"The Lord is close to the brokenhearted and saves those who are crushed in spirit." – Psalm 34:18

Prayer:

"Dear God, protect me from harm and help me to be brave enough to speak up when I'm uncomfortable. Help me find people who will keep me safe. Help me to continue to speak the truth until the right people listen. Amen."

Topic 32: Secrets and Trust

Carmen's best friend Noah told her a secret. He's been feeling really sad lately and even thought about hurting himself. Carmen promised not to tell anyone, but now she's worried about him.

What would you do?

☐ Encourage Carmen to tell a trusted adult even if it means breaking the promise.
☐ Tell Carmen to keep the secret no matter what.
☐ Ignore it and let Carmen deal with the situation.

Have you ever had to decide between keeping a promise and doing the right thing? When is it okay to tell someone's secret?

Write how Carmen feels, wanting to help Noah but unsure how.

What does the Bible say?

"Speak up for those who cannot speak for themselves." – Proverbs 31:8

Prayer:

"Dear God, help me know when it's right to keep a secret and when it's important to speak up to protect someone. Give me the courage to do what's right. Amen."

Topic 33: Suicidal Thoughts

Kayla's friend Carla has been saying things like, "I don't think I matter," and "I wish I could disappear." Kayla is scared for her friend but doesn't know how to help.

What would you do?

- ☐ Encourage Kayla to tell an adult she trusts so they can help Carla.
- ☐ Tell Kayla to ignore it because Carla just wants attention.
- ☐ Let Kayla deal with it on her own, you don't know Carla that well.

What do you know about suicide?

Describe how Kayla might feel hearing these things from her friend and feeling conflicted about wanting to reach out for help.

What does the Bible say?

"The Lord is my light and my salvation; whom shall I fear?" – Psalm 27:1

Prayer:

"Dear God, help me to listen and support my friends when they are feeling sad. Help me to seek support if I ever have thoughts of suicide. I know that the enemy will put thoughts in my head and I don't have to act on them. Show me how to get help when there is danger. Amen."

Topic 34: Bullying

Kingston has been picking on Caden for the way he talks. Caden doesn't know how to make it stop and feels like he's alone. Caden has a speech impediment and now he is afraid to read out loud in class. You notice how the bullying is affecting Caden and you want to do something, but you're not sure how to help.

What would you do?

- ☐ Encourage Caden to tell a teacher or trusted adult about the bullying.
- ☐ Tell Kingston that it's not right to make fun of someone's differences.
- ☐ Join in with Kingston because you don't want to be bullied either.

What can you do to feel more confident despite your insecurities?

Describe how Caden might feel, insecure and upset every day.

What does the Bible say?

"Do to others as you would have them do to you." – Luke 6:31

Prayer:

"Dear God, help me to be kind to everyone and stand up for those who are being bullied. Teach me to speak up when I see wrong and show love to others. Amen."

Topic 35: Different Types of Families

Chad feels sad sometimes because his family is different from his friends'. His friends continue to make jokes about dads going out for milk and never coming back. His mom and dad don't live together, and he's not sure how to explain that to his classmates who keep asking him about his dad.

What would you do?

- ☐ Tell Chad that families come in all shapes and sizes, and that's okay, because God loves him.
- ☐ Tell Chad to lie about his family so no one knows.
- ☐ Avoid talking about it because family situations are too personal.

Have you ever felt ashamed because of your family? Describe it.

Describe how Chad might feel having to explain something hard.

What does the Bible say?

"Father of the fatherless and protector of widows is God in his holy habitation"– Psalm 68:5

Prayer:

"Dear God, thank you for my family, even when it's different from others'. Thank you for being the Father of the fatherless. Help me to understand that love makes a family, not just who lives in my house. Amen."

1. Be polite to others.
2. Clean up after yourself.
3. Help with household chores.
4. Respect the quiet.
5. Communicate openly.
6. Respect others' privacy.
7. Follow the house rules.
8. Keep shared spaces clean.
9. Conserve resources.
10. Take responsibility for your actions.

www.chatterboxtherapists.com

Topic 36: A Student with Alopecia

Annette just found out that Charmen has an illness called Alopecia, and it makes her hair fall out. Charmen doesn't talk much about it, and Annette isn't sure if she should ask about it or not.

What would you do?

- ☐ Encourage Annette to be kind and let Charmen talk when she's ready.
- ☐ Tell Annette to ignore it because it's too complicated.
- ☐ Avoid talking to Charmen because Alopecia is contagious.

How would you approach asking about something that is sensitive to your friend?

Describe how Carmen might feel, unsure of who to trust with her medical diagnosis.

What does the Bible say?

"When you help those who are suffering, you are also helping the Lord. He will take notice of your kindness and generosity." – Proverbs 19:17

Prayer:

"Dear God, help me to be kind and patient with others, especially when they are going through tough times. Show me how to be a friend who listens and cares. Amen."

Topic 37: A Displaced Student

Caden's new friend Corey confided in him that he and his family have been evicted and all of his things were placed outside and he's devastated. Caden doesn't know how to help Corey or what to say.

What would you do?

- ☐ Encourage Caden to be a good friend and offer support by asking the school counselor for some resources for Corey.
- ☐ Tell Caden to avoid Corey because it's too awkward.
- ☐ Let Caden feel sorry for Corey but not do anything.

What do you think it would be like to focus in school while being unhoused?

Write how Corey might feel, losing everything that he owned.

What does the Bible say?

"Whoever is kind to the poor lends to the LORD, and he will reward them for what they have done." Proverbs 19:17

211

I need help...

- paying my bills
- caregiver resources
- contacting a local 211

01 FOOD

DO YOU NEED HELP WITH FOOD? CONTACT 211 FOR SUPPORT.

Housing 02

DO YOU NEED HELP FINDING A HOME? IF YOU NEED HELP FINDING SOMEEWHERE TO LIVE, CALL 211.

03

Health

DO YOU KNOW SOMEONE THAT NEEDS HELP WITH ADDICTION, OR SUBSTANCE ABUSE? CALL 211

MENTAL HEALTH SERVICES

MEDICAL SERVICES

WWW.CHATTERBOXTHERAPISTS.COM

Topic 38: You had One Job

Mark’s parents left him home alone overnight for the first time. His parents told him not to have company and to stay home until they get back. Mark posts on social media that he is home alone and he’s going to have a few friends over. Mark invited you and three other friends over. You know that he’s not supposed to have company.

What would you do?

☐ Encourage Mark to delete the posts from social media and cancel the get together.

☐ Tell Mark that you will come for an hour, but you have to get home after that.

☐ Go to Mark's house and enjoy yourself, you only live once.

Describe the consequences that you experienced due to a bad choice.

What are some things that could happen if Mark has company?

What does the Bible say?

“Honor your father and your mother, so that you may live long in the land the LORD your God is giving you.” – Exodus 20:12

Prayer:

“Dear God, help me to listen to my parents so that my days will be long. Teach me to make good choices and honor you in all I do. Amen.”

6 CRITICAL THINKINGSKILLS

To Improve Media Literacy

1 Seek Diverse Perspectives

Algorithms on social media platforms feed us information that aligns with our own views. We must intentionally seek out perspectives that differ from our own. This allows us to see alternative ideas, improves understanding, and creates a more accurate picture of the world we live in.

2 Ask Questions

Be curious about the world and people around you. Questions help us clarify, explore, and evaluate information. Ask yourself: What is the purpose of this post? Does the author back up their claims with reliable evidence? Are there any alternative arguments or explanations?

3 Engage in Conversation

Respectful and constructive dialogue with others can lead to collaboration and an exchange of ideas. Conversations with others help us challenge our assumptions and get feedback to our own questions and opinions.

4 Self-Reflect

We often interpret media through our own lens of personal experiences and beliefs. It is important to examine and evaluate our thoughts and values. Introspection gives us insight into our thinking process.

5 Educate Yourself

We can continuously become more knowledgeable. Educating ourselves allows personal growth, increases self-confidence, and enhances curiosity. When we consume media, we should ask ourselves: What can I learn from this? How will I use this information?

6 Apply Your Learning

We are bombarded with media every day, so we need to be mindful of what media we give our time and attention to. When we apply our skills to real-word situations, it allows us to test our understanding of concepts, apply logic, and be creative in our thinking.

WWW.CHATTERBOXTHERAPISTS.COM

Topic 39: Friend Comes to School with Bruises

Carmen noticed her friend Noah had bruises on his arms that he tried to hide. When Carmen asked him about it, Noah seemed nervous and changed the subject. Noah didn't come to school the next day and Carmen is worried.

What would you do?

☐ Encourage Carmen to talk to a trusted adult about her concern.
☐ Tell Carmen to ignore it since Noah didn't want to talk about it.
☐ Ask other students to see if they know what's going on with Noah.

If you noticed bruises on your friend's arms, what would you do?

Describe how Noah might feel at home and at school.

What does the Bible say?
"Rescue the weak and the needy; deliver them from the hand of the wicked." – Psalm 82:4

Prayer:
"Dear God, help me to care for my friends and speak up when something isn't right. Give me courage to ask for help when others need it. Amen."

Topic 40: Unfair Treatment by the School Security Officer

Jackson noticed that his friend Corey was treated unfairly by the school security officer, just because Corey looks different. Jackson felt upset but didn't know what to say.

What would you do?

- ☐ Encourage Jackson to tell his parents, a teacher and or principal about the situation.
- ☐ Tell Jackson to ignore it because it's not his business.
- ☐ Tell Jackson to confront the security officer directly.

Have you ever seen someone treated unfairly because they looked different? How did you feel about it?

Describe how Corey might feel judged for no reason.

What does the Bible say?
"Do not judge, or you too will be judged." – Matthew 7:1

Prayer:
"Dear God, help me to see others as you see them and stand up against unfair treatment. Teach me to love everyone that you love, no matter how different they are. Amen."

Topic 41: The Math's Not Mathing

Antonio failed his math test and now he's worried about his grades. He's embarrassed, because he's known as the "smart kid" in class. His teacher is willing to tutor him in the mornings before class, but he doesn't want his friends to see him getting tutored. He asks you for advice about what he could do.

What would you do?

- ☐ Encourage Antonio to ask the teacher for help and get tutoring, because no one knows everything.
- ☐ Tell Antonio to hide the fact that he is failing in math to avoid getting bullied.
- ☐ Ignore the situation because Antonio was a, "know it all."

What is more important, getting the help that you need, or other people's opinions about you getting the help that you need?

Describe how Antonio feels, and why you think he feels that way.

What does the Bible say?

"Trust in the Lord with all your heart and lean not on your own understanding." – Proverbs 3:5

Prayer:

"Dear God, help me to do my best in school and trust you to guide me when I feel like giving up. Amen."

What is Maths Anxiety?

Maths anxiety is the sense of fear or stress that arises when faced with mathematical tasks. This feeling can lead to nervousness, frustration, or a sense of being overwhelmed.

The signs

- Feeling nervous before maths lessons
- Avoiding maths homework or practice
- Panic or frustration when solving problems

Overcoming Maths Anxiety

- Challenge negative thoughts
- Master the basics
- Break down the problem
- Practice maths daily
- Ask for help if you need
- Breathe and Relax
- Celebrate progress

Topic 42: How Would They Know?

Ramona is in charge of making copies of the tests for her third period class. She notices that the teacher accidentally gave her the answer key to the next math exam. She makes a few copies and hides them in her notebook. She offers you a copy during lunch. You know that you can pass the exam if you study. She hands the answer key to you...

What would you do?

- ☐ Accept the answer key from Ramona to avoid offending her, but don't use it, study for the exam.
- ☐ Reject the answer key and tell Ramona what you think about her doing this.
- ☐ Accept the answer key from Ramona and use it for the next exam.

How do you feel about cheating?

What are some consequences that Ramona could experience by copying the answers to the next math exam?

What does the Bible say?

"Whoever walks in integrity walks securely, but whoever takes crooked paths will be found out." – Proverbs 10:9

Prayer:

"Dear God, help me to be honest and work hard, even when it's tempting to take shortcuts. Teach me to trust in doing what's right. Amen."

6 Effective Ways

To Study better

1

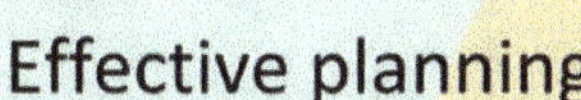

Effective planning

Create a study schedule that breaks down your tasks into manageable sessions, ensuring a balance between subjects and topics

2 Active Learning

Engage actively with the material through methods like summarizing information, teaching concepts to others, and participating in discussions.

3 Varied study methods

Utilize different study techniques, such as reading, note-taking, flashcards, and practice questions, to reinforce learning through various approaches.

4

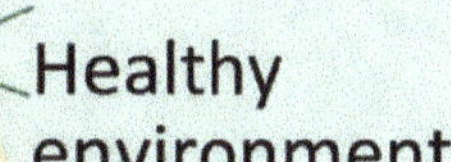

Healthy environment

Choose a comfortable and well-lit study environment, minimizing distractions to enhance focus and concentration.

5

Regular breaks

Take short breaks during study sessions to prevent mental fatigue and maintain overall productivity.

Self-Assessment

Regularly evaluate your understanding of the material through self-assessment tools, quizzes, or practice exams to identify areas that need further review.

Topic 43: Crushed

Caden didn't finish his homework and now he's asking Carmen to let him copy hers before class starts. No one is around. Carmen worked very hard on her homework, but she's conflicted because she has a crush on Caden, and this is the first time he's spoken to her.

What do you think Carmen could do?

- ☐ Encourage Caden to finish his own homework.
- ☐ Let Caden copy the homework just this once.
- ☐ Tell Caden that he owes her something if he copies from her homework.

Have you ever copied homework or been asked to share yours? What did you do?

How do you think Carmen felt to have her crush talk to her for the first time? Do you think she knows that he was just trying to copy her work?

What does the Bible say?

"Whoever can be trusted with very little can also be trusted with much." – Luke 16:10

Prayer:

"Dear God, help me to set boundaries and not allow people to use me. Teach me to value honesty and responsibility. Help me to discern the difference between true friends and fake ones. Amen."

Topic 44: Closed Mouths Don't Get Fed

Annette feels shy in class, so she never asks questions even when she doesn't understand. Now she's falling behind but she's afraid to ask her teacher for help. She has been hiding her grades from her mom and she doesn't want to get her phone taken away for failing the class. Annette see's you are asking for help from the teacher and later she asks you to help her study.

What would you do?

- ☐ Encourage Annette to raise her hand and ask the teacher for help.
- ☐ Tell Annette to keep quiet and try to figure it out on her own.
- ☐ Offer to explain the lessons to Annette after class.

Have you ever been too shy to ask for help when you needed it? What was the outcome of that situation?

How do you think Annette feels, being too scared to speak up?

What does the Bible say?
"Ask and it will be given to you; seek and you will find." – Matthew 7:7

Prayer:
"Dear God, help me to be brave enough to ask for help when I need it. Remind me that it's okay not to know everything. Amen."

Topic 45: Feeling Lost

Carter has been feeling lost lately. He doesn't know what he's good at, and he feels like everyone else has it all figured out. He's been trying to figure out who he is and it's stressing him out. He's almost 13 years old and he feels like he should feel different than when he was just 12. You see him sitting alone in the lunchroom.

What would you do?

- ☐ Encourage Carter to try new things until he finds what he enjoys.
- ☐ Tell Carter to give up because it's too hard to figure out.
- ☐ Ignore it because everyone feels lost sometimes and he's too young to care.

How do you feel about getting older?

How do you think Carter feels about turning 13?

What does the Bible say?
"For I know the plans I have for you," declares the Lord, "plans to prosper you and not to harm you." – Jeremiah 29:11

Prayer:
"Dear God, guide me when I feel lost and unsure of myself. Show me your plan for my life and help me trust in your guidance. Amen."

NAME: ______________ DATE: __________

MY    GOAL PLANNER

SPECIFIC

What exactly do I want to accomplish?

MEASURABLE

How will I know when I meet my goal?

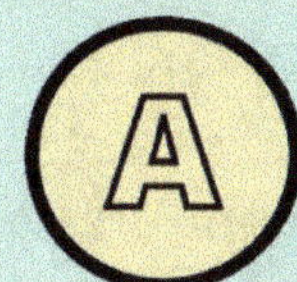

ATTAINABLE

Is it possible to meet this goal with effort by my timeline?

RELEVANT

Is this goal worth working hard to accomplish? Does it help me with my long term goals?

TIMELY

What is the deadline I have set to meet this goal?

WWW.CHATTERBOXTHERAPISTS.COM

Topic 46: Rocket Science

Chase has been struggling with science, and now he feels like he's behind because he can't understand the lessons like his friends do. When he looks at the directions for the science experiments it seems like the words are moving on the page. He knows that to pass this class he has to complete a project for the competition, so he chose the Rocket Launch Project. He's excited about it, and nervous at the same time. You also chose the Rocket Launch Project and the winner gets a trophy and an opportunity to show their project off at the next science fair. Chase is your friend and neighbor, and he asked you for help with his project.

What would you do?

- ☐ Encourage Chase to ask for extra help from the teacher.
- ☐ Tell Chase he's not stupid and that everyone struggles sometimes, he just needs to work harder.
- ☐ Help Chase finish his project and risk losing the competition.

Have you ever felt like you weren't smart enough to understand something? Describe how that felt for you.

What does the Bible say?

"If any of you lacks wisdom, you should ask God, who gives generously to all without finding fault." – James 1:5

Prayer:

"Dear God, help me to help my friends when they are struggling the way that You help me. Teach me that what's for me is for me and no one can block my blessings. Amen."

Dream

BIG

Topic 47: Negative Thoughts

Kingston has been thinking negative things about himself lately, like "I'm not good enough" or "No one cares about me." He doesn't know how to make these thoughts stop.

What would you do?

- ☐ Encourage Kingston to talk to someone about his feelings.
- ☐ Tell Kingston to ignore it and hope the thoughts go away.
- ☐ Tell Kingston to distract himself with other activities.

Have you ever had negative thoughts that made you feel bad about yourself? Describe it and write the opposite of the negative thoughts that you've had about yourself. If you read the positive statements about yourself daily in the mirror, you will begin to feel better about who you are. Try it out.

Negative Thoughts	Positive Thoughts

How do you think Kingston feels about being trapped in his own mind?

What does the Bible say?

"Finally, brothers and sisters, whatever is true, whatever is noble, whatever is right... think about such things." – Philippians 4:8

Prayer: "Dear God, help me to replace negative thoughts with your truth. Remind me that I am loved, valuable, and good enough in your eyes. Amen.

MINDFUL AFFIRMATIONS

POSITIVE THOUGHTS TO START YOUR DAY

I appreciate today and how I feel

I will show myself compassion

I am present in this moment

I will focus on what brings me joy

I am calm and peaceful

I welcome today's opportunities

I accept my thoughts and feelings

I am connected to what surrounds me

I am grateful for who I am

Topic 48: Soggy Sleepover

You invited Curtis to his first sleepover, but Curtis feels nervous about sleeping away from home. Curtis wakes up in the middle of the night and his pajamas are wet and so are your sleeping bags. Curtis comes out of the bathroom with a different set of pajamas on, and he looks terrified that you've discovered his secret.

What would you do?

☐ Tell Curtis that he needs to ask to go home early since he had an accident in your room at his big age.

☐ Tell Curtis that it's okay, help him wash his sleeping bag and pajamas, and ask him to sleep on your bottom bunk bed where it's dry.

☐ Look at Curtis like he has the plague and tell your friends to stay away from him because he wet the bed.

Have you ever had an accident? How could you help your friends feel comfortable even when they do something that embarrasses them?

What would you do if you were Curtis and you had an accident at your friend's house?

What does the Bible say?

"When I am afraid, I put my trust in you." – Psalm 56:3

Prayer: "Dear God, help me to be brave when I try new things and trust that you are with me wherever I go. Help me to be kind to my friends when they do something that embarrasses them. Amen."

WHAT MAKES A GOOD FRIEND?

1

TRUSTWORTHINESS

A good friend keeps their promises and respects your secrets unless there is a risk of that friend getting harmed. A good friend will have integrity, be honest and fair. If someone doesn't have good values, can they be a good friend?

2

KINDNESS

They are caring, supportive, and treat you with compassion. They care about your feelings and the will validate your experience, even if they disagree with your decision. They will let you know what they think you could have done in a respectful way.

3

HONESTY

A good friend tells the truth, even when it's hard, but always in a loving way. They will talk to you in private about things that may be sensitive to you and they would not try to embarrass you.

4

RELIABILITY

They show up when you need them and are dependable during both good and bad times.

5

RESPECT

A good friend values your opinions, boundaries, and feelings, even if they are different from their own. They want what's best for you and they won't encourage you to do something that could get you in trouble. They want what's best for you.

WWW.CHATTERBOXTHERAPISTS.COM

LIST CHARACTERISTICS THAT YOU LOOK FOR IN A FRIEND

1

2

3

4

5

WHAT MAKES YOU A GOOD FRIEND?

1

2

3

4

5

WWW.CHATTERBOXTHERAPISTS.COM

Topic 49: Trying New Foods

Annette invited you over for dinner, her family is having a special meal with new foods that you never tried before. You're not sure if you'll like it but you don't want to be rude.

What would you do?

☐ Try a small bite of each new food to see if you like it.

☐ Tell Annette that you will only eat what you know you like and you'll skip the rest.

☐ Tell Annette to politely tell her family you're not interested in trying new things.

What was a food that you didn't think you'd like, but you liked it once you tried it?

Think about how Annette feels knowing that you may not like her family's food?

What does the Bible say?

"So whether you eat or drink or whatever you do, do it all for the glory of God." – 1 Corinthians 10:31

Prayer:

"Dear God, help me to be open to new experiences and remind me that trying new things can be fun as long as it glorifies You. Amen."

Topic 50: Asking for Permission

Jackson really wants to go to a friend's house after school to see his new game console, but he knows he has to ask for permission first. He's worried his parents might say no, because they never let him go to anyone's house until they meet his friend's parents. His parents aren't home and his friend's house is literally right up the street. They won't know if he pops in and takes a peek.

What would you do?

- ☐ Call your parents to ask politely and accept whatever answer your parents give.
- ☐ Go without asking because it's easier to ask for forgiveness than permission, and they may not even find out anyway.
- ☐ Ask your parents and get mad if they say no.

Have you ever been afraid to ask for permission/ What happened?

Describe how Jackson feels, anxious but knowing he needs to do the right thing.

What does the Bible say?

"Children, obey your parents in everything, for this pleases the Lord." – Colossians 3:20

Prayer: "Dear God, help me to ask for permission and respect the decisions of those in charge, knowing that they want what's best for me. Amen."

mindfulness helps us:

Balance our emotions

Show kindness

Find calm

Focus and observe

Spark our curiosity

Build confidence

Learn compassion

Topic 51: When They Tell You No

Kayla asked her parents if she could go to a party, but they said no. Now she feels frustrated and doesn't know how to handle it. She wants to sneak out and go anyway, but that is super risky. She is thinking about telling her parents that she is going to sleepover at your house but she'll go to the party instead. She calls you and asks you if you could cover for her.

What would you do?

☐ Encourage Kayla not to go to the party, and ask her to come over for real.
☐ Tell Kayla that you will cover for her this one time, but she will owe you one.
☐ Tell Kayla to sneak out to the party without them knowing.

Have you ever been upset when you didn't get your way? How do you feel when your parents tell you no?

Why do your parents tell you "no" sometimes?

What does the Bible say?

"Trust in the Lord with all your heart and lean not on your own understanding." – Proverbs 3:5

Prayer:

"Dear God, help me to accept when things don't go my way and trust that you have a plan, even when I don't understand. Amen."

Topic 52: Changing Your Mind

Caden told his friend Chase he would go with him to confront a bully after school, but now he's not sure if he wants to. He's afraid to tell Chase that he's changed his mind, because he doesn't want to be accused of backing out because he's scared. He just doesn't want to get suspended and get in trouble.

What would you do?

- ☐ Encourage Caden to be honest with Chase and explain why he changed his mind.
- ☐ Tell Caden to go along with it, even if he doesn't want to anymore.
- ☐ Ignore it because Chase will focus on you if you give your opinion.

Have you ever changed your mind and felt bad about it because someone else was counting on you?

Describe how Caden feels, worried about disappointing his friend.

What does the Bible say? "Make no friendship with a man given to anger, nor go with a wrathful man, lest you learn his ways and entangle yourself in a snare."-Proverbs 22:24-25

Prayer: "Dear God, help me to be honest with others and clear about my decisions, even when it's hard. Thank you for letting me know that it's okay to change my mind and stand on what I believe. Amen."

Topic 53: Feeling Embarrassed

Corey tripped on the stage during his eighth-grade graduation and everyone saw him. Now he finds himself replaying his most embarrassing moments repeatedly in his mind. He has begun to speak negatively about himself, and he has become withdrawn. It's been two weeks since school let out. He lives next door, and you notice that he hasn't come outside yet.

What would you do?

- ☐ Encourage Corey to laugh it off and realize everyone makes mistakes.
- ☐ Tell Corey to hide in his bedroom until everyone forgets.
- ☐ Tell Corey that it's normal to feel embarrassed sometimes but talk to the school counselor about his feelings.

Have you ever been embarrassed in front of others and couldn't stop thinking about it? Describe it below.

What type of support would you like to receive for ruminating thoughts?

What does the Bible say? "Do not be anxious about anything, but in every situation, by prayer and petition, with thanksgiving, present your requests to God. And the peace of God, which transcends all understanding, will guard your hearts and your minds in Christ Jesus." Philippians 4:6-7

Prayer: "Dear God, help me to let go of embarrassment and focus on who you say I am, not what others think of me. Amen."

Topic 54: Money Issues

Antonio overheard his parents talking about money issues. Now he feels worried but doesn't know how to talk to them about his feelings. He was going to ask for money to go to homecoming this weekend, but now he's worried that they may not be able to afford it. The next morning both of his parents looked normal, but he was still stressed. When they asked him to share his thoughts, he said that he was okay.

What would you do?

- ☐ Encourage Antonio to ask his parents how he can help and share his feelings.
- ☐ Tell Antonio to ignore it because it's not his problem.
- ☐ Tell Antonio to find a way to make money to help his family.

Have you ever worried about money or something that felt out of your control? What did you do?

What does the Bible say?

"And my God will meet all your needs according to the riches of his glory in Christ Jesus." – Philippians 4:19

Prayer:

"Dear God, help me to trust you to provide for my family and remind me that you will always take care of us. Amen."

Topic 55: Grief and Loss

Carmen's grandmother passed away, and now Carmen feels sad all the time. She doesn't know how to talk about her feelings and worries about crying in front of others. During class Carmen was quiet and withdrawn which was unusual for her. You look over and you see that she has her head down on her desk and she appears to be crying.

What would you do?

☐ Encourage Carmen to talk about her feelings with someone she can trust..

☐ Tell Carmen to bottle up her feelings and not talk about them.

☐ Tell Carmen to distract herself and hope the sadness goes away.

Can you grieve something other than the loss of a loved one? What type of things could be lost or changed?

Have you ever grieved anything? Describe it. (Examples: Friendships, schools, neighborhoods, sentimental items, et

What does the Bible say?

"The Lord is close to the brokenhearted and saves those who are crushed in spirit." – Psalm 34:18

Prayer:

"Dear God, comfort me in times of grief and remind me that you are always near, even in sadness. Amen."

IDENTIFYING MY EMOTIONS

WWW.CHATTERBOXTHERAPISTS.COM

Topic 56: Finders Keepers

Slone found money on the ground at school. Instead of turning it in, she decided to keep it, even though he knew it wasn't his. He later overhears that the one teacher that gave him a "C" in his class was the one that lost the money. She notices that you've been watching her this whole time. She asks you if you would like some money, but you can't tell anyone.

What would you do?

☐ Encourage Slone to return the money to the office and do the right thing.

☐ Tell Slone it's okay to keep it because no one will notice.

☐ Tell Slone to share the money with her friends secretly.

Have you ever found something that didn't belong to you and didn't know what to do?

How would you feel if you lost something and someone kept it for themselves?

What does the Bible say?

"You shall not steal." – Exodus 20:15

Prayer:

"Dear God, help me to be honest and return what isn't mine, even when no one else is watching. Amen."

Topic 57: Parents with Mental Illness

Caden's mom has been acting differently, sometimes she seems sad and other times she's angry. Caden doesn't understand what's going on and feels scared. He's never seen his mother behave this way and now he wants to spend more time at your home with you and your parents because they are kind to him, and he trusts them.

What would you do?

- ☐ Encourage Caden to ask a trusted adult for help like your parents.
- ☐ Tell Caden to ignore it and hope things get better.
- ☐ Tell Caden it's not his place to worry about his mom's feelings.

Have you ever felt confused or scared because of how someone close to you was acting? What happened?

Describe how Caden feels, confused and unsure of how to handle it.

What does the Bible say?

"Cast all your anxiety on him because he cares for you." – 1 Peter 5:7

Prayer:

"Dear God, help me to trust you when I feel scared or confused. Help my mom feel better and give us peace. Amen."

SELF LOVE AND MENTAL HEALTH

01

Self-love is a practice of nurturing and valuing oneself. It includes accepting both strengths and weaknesses and prioritizing self-care.

03

Self-love involves setting healthy boundaries, saying no when necessary, and prioritizing one's own needs and well-being without guilt.

02

Practicing self-love can improve mental health by boosting self-esteem, self-confidence, and resilience in the face of challenges.

Self-love includes practicing self-compassion and treating oneself with kindness and understanding during difficult times or when facing setbacks.

04

WWW.CHATTERBOXTHERAPISTS.COM

Topic 58: Incarcerated Parents

Jamie hasn't seen his dad in a long time because he's in jail. He feels embarrassed and doesn't know how to talk to his friends about it. His father will be released soon and he's afraid of what people will think about him and his family. He wants people to know what really happened: his dad was a victim who defended himself, but they arrested him anyway. He loves his dad and he's excited for him to come home, but he feels guilty about feeling embarrassed at the same time.

What would you do?

- ☐ Encourage Jamie to talk to his parents to get an idea about how his family wants to handle this matter..
- ☐ Tell Jamie to keep it a secret so no one finds out.
- ☐ Tell Jamie to act like nothing's wrong, even though it bothers him.

Have you ever had a secret or situation you were embarrassed to talk about? Describe how that felt for you.

Describe how Jamie feels, wanting to hide his situation but also wanting to share the truth.

What does the Bible say?

"The Lord hears the needy and does not despise his captive people." – Psalm 69:33

Prayer: "Dear God, help me to feel your love even when things are tough. Help me to talk to someone who cares about me. Amen."

Topic 59: Absent Parents

Kayla's dad never comes to her school events or her birthday. She feels sad because she wishes he would be more involved in her life. She wants to call him and tell him how she feels, but she's afraid that he will reject her. She asks you for advice...

What would you do?

☐ Encourage Kayla to talk to her mom or another adult about her feelings, before calling her dad.

☐ Tell Kayla it doesn't matter and she should get over it.

☐ Tell Kayla to pretend it doesn't bother her, even though it does.

Have you ever felt sad because someone you care about wasn't there for you?

Describe how Kayla feels, missing her dad and feeling disappointed.

What does the Bible say?

"Even if my father and mother abandon me, the Lord will hold me close." – Psalm 27:10

Prayer:

"Dear God, help me to know that you are always there for me, even when people in my life are not. Amen."

Topic 60: Blended Families

Annette's mom got remarried, and now she has two stepbrothers. She's having trouble getting along with them and feels left out. She's used to her mother showing her more attention, but now she has to share her mother with three additional people. Annette would like to spend some alone time with her mom because she misses her. She asked you to help her come up with what to say to her mom.

What would you do?

- ☐ Encourage Annette to talk to her mom about how she feels and try try to get to know her stepbrothers better.
- ☐ Help Annette create a card for her mom expressing how much she misses her, with a proposed day and time for them to hang out alone.
- ☐ Tell Annette to ignore her stepbrothers and not try to get along.

Have you ever had to adjust to a big change in your family?

If not, think about how Annette feels, trying to find her place.

What does the Bible say?

"How good and pleasant it is when God's people live together in unity!" – Psalm 133:1

Prayer:

"Dear God, help me to find peace and understanding in my new family. Help us learn to get along and love each other. Amen."

Respect others

Always show kindness and respect to family members and guests.

Pitch In

Contribute to family well-being by helping with household chores.

Talk to Us

Please share your thoughts, feelings, and concerns with us. We are here to listen and support you.

Follow House Rules

Please follow the household rules for harmony and safety.

Be Mindful of Resources

To save energy, remember to turn off lights and appliances when not in use.

WWW.CHATTERBOXTHERAPISTS.COM

Topic 61: Feeling Neglected

Slone feels like her parents never have time for her because they're always busy with work and taking care of her younger brother. Grace notices that Slone has been working hard in school to get the best grades to show her parents and gain their approval. Grace understands that parents get caught up in life sometimes because she remembers feeling this way, but when she talked to her parents, they apologized and then explained that they thought Grace didn't need them as much. Grace let them know that she still needs them to show her attention and spend time with her and they become more intentional about doing just that.

What would you do?

- ☐ Encourage Slone to talk to her parents about spending more time together.
- ☐ Tell Slone that good grades will be the key to happiness.
- ☐ Tell Slone to stay quiet and not bother her parents.

Have you ever felt like people were too busy to spend time with you? How did that make you feel?

Explain how it feels to feel lonely and left out.

What does the Bible say?

"The Lord is close to the brokenhearted and saves those who are crushed in spirit." – Psalm 34:18

Prayer: "Dear God, help me to feel your love and remind my parents how much I need their time and attention. Amen."

I AM **LOVED**

I AM **SMART**

I AM **KIND**

I AM **CAPABLE**

I AM **BRAVE**

I AM **ENOUGH**

Topic 62: Mom's Favorite Child

Chase feels like his mom always favors his younger sister and never gives him the same attention. It makes him feel jealous and hurt. He started to become rude to his little sister because he blames her for the way his parents treat him. You see him push her down when they are outside and you ask them about what happened. He told you that he doesn't have to be nice to someone that ruined his life. You and Chase talk about after you comfort his little sister and take her back inside of her house.

What could Chase do?

- ☐ Talk to his mom about how he feels about being the older brother who no longer receives the time he used to get.
- ☐ Tell Chase to keep quiet and deal with it because he's getting older and this is what is supposed to happen.
- ☐ Tell Chase to act out so he can get more attention.

Have you ever felt like someone else was getting more attention than you? How would you describe that feeling?

What does the Bible say?

"Love each other as I have loved you." – John 15:12

Prayer:

"Dear God, help me to love my family even when I feel left out. Help me to talk about my feelings in a kind way. Amen."

Topic 63: Losing a Sibling

Noah's older brother passed away, and now he feels really sad and doesn't know how to handle the loss. He feels like no one understands what he's going through. You spent time with Noah and his older brother and you know that they were really close. Noah can hardly get through one day without silently crying in class. When you ask him what's wrong, he simply says, "You wouldn't understand."

What would you do?

- ☐ Encourage Noah that you don't understand his feelings but he's welcome to share them with you and with an adult that he trusts.
- ☐ Tell Noah that you do understand because you spent time with his brother as well.
- ☐ Tell Noah to pretend he's okay so people don't ask questions.

Have you ever experienced the loss of someone close to you? How did that make you feel? Who did you talk to about your feelings?

Write how Noah feels, heartbroken and grieving.

What does the Bible say?

"The Lord is close to the brokenhearted and saves those who are crushed in spirit." – Psalm 34:18

Prayer:

"Dear God, comfort me in my sadness and remind me that you are with me, even in my darkest times. Amen."

Topic 64: Being the Youngest Child

Carmen is the youngest in her family, and she often feels like her older siblings don't take her seriously. She wants to be treated more fairly, but they never let her join in when they are having fun or talking about something serious that she knows about.

What would you do?

☐ Encourage Carmen to talk to her siblings about how she feels and ask them to include her more.

☐ Tell Carmen to stay quiet because there's nothing she can do, since she's the youngest child.

☐ Tell Carmen to interrupt her siblings and push herself into their space to gain their respect.

What is something that you wish adults understood about you although you are young?

Express how it feels wanting to be included and respected.

What does the Bible say?

"Don't let anyone look down on you because you are young." – 1 Timothy 4:12

Prayer:

"Dear God, help me to feel confident in who I am, no matter my age, and help me to speak up when I feel left out. Amen."

Topic 65: Being the Middle Child

Corey is the middle child and feels like he's always overlooked between his older and younger siblings. He feels invisible sometimes. He stays out of the way at home, in class and during recess.

What would you do?

- ☐ Invite Corey to hang out with you and your friends so that he will feel included.
- ☐ Tell Corey to keep quiet because it won't change anything at home, he's the middle child.
- ☐ Tell Corey to change his personality so that his family will care about him more.

Have you ever felt invisible or ignored because of your position in the family? Describe your experience below.

Describe how Corey feels, caught in the middle and feeling overlooked.

What does the Bible say?

"I praise you because I am fearfully and wonderfully made." – Psalm 139:14

Prayer:

"Dear God, help me to know that I am important and valued, even when I feel left out. Amen."

Topic 66: Being the Oldest Child

Annette is the oldest child and feels a lot of pressure to set a good example for her younger siblings, which is difficult because she feels like she's not able to make mistakes. This pressure has caused her to feel anxious about everything she does. You notice that she is becoming more stressed about having to make decisions because she's afraid of making the wrong one. She asks you to help her choose a topic for her history assignment because she can't seem to make any decisions.

What would you do?

- ☐ Encourage Annette to talk to her parents about how much responsibility she feels.
- ☐ Tell Annette to stop being the perfect child for her siblings because no one is perfect.
- ☐ Tell Annette to get angry with her siblings for not doing more.

What are reasonable expectations for someone your age?

What does the Bible say?

"Come to me, all you who are weary and burdened, and I will give you rest." – Matthew 11:28

Prayer:

"Dear God, help me to manage my responsibilities and give me the strength to ask for help when I need it. Amen."

Topic 67: Monthly Mishap

Mya is sitting behind her friend Sarah in class when she notices that Sarah has started her period, and there's a spot on her chair. Sarah doesn't seem to know what's happened, and no one else has noticed.

What would you do?

- ☐ Quietly let Sarah know what's going on and offer to get her jacket to tie around her waist so that she can go to the restroom.
- ☐ Ignore it and hope someone else tells her, because it's not your business and Sarah has never spoken to you before. .
- ☐ Tell the whole class and make a joke about it, since you get picked on for things you can't control.

What is the most embarrassing thing that could happen to you in front of your classmates?

How you can be kind to classmates and friends who are experiencing something embarrassing.

What does the Bible say?

"So in everything, do to others what you would have them do to you." – Matthew 7:12

Prayer: "Dear God, help me be kind and gentle when others are going through embarrassing or difficult moments. Help me to show love and respect in every situation. Amen."

Topic 68: Weird and Embarrassing Changes

Eric has been noticing changes in his body lately, and he feels really awkward and embarrassed about it. He's not sure if his friends are going through the same thing, and he doesn't know who to talk to. He has a best friend his age, but he doesn't know if what he is feeling is normal because they never talk about stuff that's happening with their bodies.

What could Eric do?

- ☐ Eric could talk to someone he trusts, like a parent, about what's happening to his body before asking his friend.
- ☐ Tell Eric to google what's happening to his body and stay quiet because it's too embarrassing to talk about.
- ☐ Laugh at Eric for feeling weird about his body changes.

Have you ever felt uncomfortable about changes in your body? Describe your feelings below.

Describe how Eric felt, confused and unsure of how to deal with it.

What does the Bible say?

"I praise you because I am fearfully and wonderfully made." – Psalm 139:14

Prayer:

"Dear God, help me to remember that the changes I'm going through are part of your plan for me. Give me the courage to talk to someone that I trust if I feel uncomfortable. Amen."

YOU CAN

DO

hard

THINGS

WWW.CHATTERBOXTHERAPISTS.COM

Topic 69: A Friend is Being Abusive to Their Pet

Timmy's friend Marvin is being rough with his dog, pulling its ears and hitting it when it doesn't listen. Timmy feels bad for the dog but isn't sure what to do.

What would you do?

☐ Encourage Timmy to tell his friend to stop being mean to the dog and explain why it's wrong.
☐ Tell Timmy to ignore it because it's not his business.
☐ Tell Timmy to join in and play rough with the dog too.

Have you ever seen someone mistreat an animal or another person? How did it make you feel?

Describe how the dog must feel being abused by someone that's supposed to protect it.

.

What does the Bible say?
"The righteous care for the needs of their animals." – Proverbs 12:10

Prayer:
"Dear God, help me to be kind to all creatures, and give me the courage to speak up when I see others being hurt. Amen."

Topic 70: Inappropriate Touching

Sade's friend Lauren tells her that her mom's boyfriend has been touching her inappropriately, and she's scared to tell anyone because she thinks she'll get in trouble. Sade feels worried and doesn't know what to do.

What would you do?

- ☐ Encourage Sade to tell a trusted adult, even if her friend doesn't want to, because it's important to keep her safe.
- ☐ Tell Sade to keep it a secret because it's not her problem.
- ☐ Tell Sade to stop being friends with Lauren because it's too complicated.

What would you do if this ever happened to you or your friend?

Describe how Laruen feels, wanting help with her situation but not sure how to get it.

What does the Bible say?

"Speak up for those who cannot speak for themselves, for the rights of all who are destitute." – Proverbs 31:8

Prayer: "Dear God, help me be brave enough to protect my friends and help those who need it by telling someone that could make a difference for them.. Give me the strength to do what's right, even when it's hard. Amen."

Topic 71: Visiting a Friend's Dirty Home

Chase goes over to his friend Billy's house for the first time and is shocked by how dirty and messy it is. Billy doesn't seem to mind, but Chase feels uncomfortable and doesn't know how to react.

What would you do?

- ☐ Encourage Chase to be kind and not judge his friend's home but to talk to a trusted adult if he feels unsafe.
- ☐ Tell Chase to stop hanging out with Billy because his house is gross.
- ☐ Tell Chase to tell all their friends about how dirty Billy's house is.

Have you ever been in a situation where you felt uncomfortable at a friend's house?

Describe how it would feel to be like Chase, surprised and unsure of how to handle it.

What does the Bible say?

"Do not judge, or you too will be judged." – Matthew 7:1

Prayer:

"Dear God, help me to be understanding and kind when I'm in situations that feel uncomfortable. Help me to treat my friends with love and respect. Amen."

Topic 72: A Parent's Addiction

Lamont's friend Heather confides in him that her dad is always drinking and sometimes yells a lot. Lamont doesn't know how to support his friend, but he knows something is wrong. Heather told Lamont that she has started to experiment with alcohol. Lamont comes to you for support, because he knows that you give the best advice.

What would you do?

- ☐ Encourage Lamont to talk to a trusted adult about his concerns for Heather.
- ☐ Tell Lamont to ignore it because it's not his business and he may get Heather in trouble.
- ☐ Tell Lamont to stop being friends with Heather because her family is too complicated.

Have you ever known someone who had a tough home life? Describe what that was like?

What does the Bible say?

"Carry each other's burdens, and in this way, you will fulfill the law of Christ." – Galatians 6:2

Prayer:

"Dear God, help me to support my friends in their struggles and to seek help when needed. Give me wisdom to know how to be a good friend. Amen."

Topic 73: Vaping

Marcus walks into the school bathroom and sees another student vaping. He knows it's wrong, but he's not sure if he should tell anyone. Marcus doesn't personally know this student, but he knows that he is popular.

What would you do?

- ☐ Encourage Marcus to report the incident to a teacher or school staff member.
- ☐ Tell Marcus to stay quiet because it's none of his business.
- ☐ Tell Marcus to try vaping too because it looks cool.

Have you ever seen someone doing something that you knew was wrong? How did you handle it?

How do you feel about vaping?

What does the Bible say?

"Do not be misled: 'Bad company corrupts good character.'" – 1 Corinthians 15:33

Prayer:

"Dear God, help me to make good choices, even when others around me are doing the wrong thing. Give me the strength to speak up when I see something wrong. Amen."

Topic 74: Running Away

Heather has been feeling really overwhelmed at home and is thinking about running away. She doesn't know where she would go, but she just wants to escape. She told you about her plan to leave home, and you're worried about her.

What would you do?

- ☐ Encourage Heather to talk to a trusted adult or counselor about her feelings instead of running away.
- ☐ Tell Heather that running away is the best option if things are tough at home.
- ☐ Tell Heather to keep her feelings to herself and not bother anyone with her problems.

Have you ever felt like you wanted to run away from your problems? Describe how that felt?

Describe how Heather feels, scared and unsure of what to do.

What does the Bible say?

"The Lord is a refuge for the oppressed, a stronghold in times of trouble." – Psalm 9:9

Prayer: "Dear God, when I feel overwhelmed, remind me that I can turn to you for help. Give me the strength to seek help instead of running away from my problems. Amen."

Topic 75: Understanding Why Your Parents Are Tired

Billy notices that his parents are always tired and don't seem to have much time to play with him anymore. He feels upset because he misses spending time with them. They mentioned that they would need to put in some extra time at work to pay off student loan debt. Billy begins to resent the lack of time his parents are spending with him. He noticed that when he gets in trouble at school one of his parents has to come to the school to pick him up. He sees this as a win, even if they are frustrated with him.

What would you do?

- ☐ Encourage Billy to talk to his parents and ask them if they can plan a special time together.
- ☐ Tell Billy to keep quiet because his parents are too busy to care.
- ☐ Tell Billy to keep acting out so his parents will notice him more.

How can you help your family get through tough times?

How do you think Billy's parents feel, having to work extra hours, and leave to pick up Billy from school, because he's acting out.

What does the Bible say?

"Come to me, all you who are weary and burdened, and I will give you rest." – Matthew 11:28

Prayer: "Dear God, help me to be patient and understanding when my parents are tired. Help us find time to spend together and strengthen our relationship. Amen."

Topic 76: What Are Bills?

Mya hears her parents talking about bills and debt, but she doesn't really understand what they mean. She wonders why it seems to cause so much stress in her home. She notices her parents arguing which is new for them. She's worried that they may get a divorce, because three of her friends' parents are divorced and all of them said that their parents were fighting over money.

What would you do?

☐ Encourage Mya to ask her parents to explain what's going on and ask them to talk about it.
☐ Tell Mya to ignore it because she's too young to worry about bills and divorce.
☐ Tell Mya to prepare to have two homes because her parents are getting a divorce.

What do you know about paying bills?

How do you think Mya feels, confused and curious.

What does the Bible say?

"Two are better than one, because they have a good return for their labor: If either of them falls down, one can help the other up." – Ecclesiastes 4:9-12

Prayer: "Dear God, help me to understand the importance of managing money wisely. Guide me to be responsible with finances when I grow older. Please help me to communicate well with my loved ones. Amen."

Topic 77: What is Debt?

Eric overhears his parents talking about debt and how hard it is to pay it off. He feels worried about what it means for his family and wants to understand more. He has been seeking answers about debt and he learned that debt is owing money to someone for a service or items that must be paid back within a certain amount of time.

What would you do?

- ☐ Encourage Eric to ask his parents to explain debt and what it means for their family's future.
- ☐ Tell Eric to keep quiet and not ask questions because it's not his business.
- ☐ Tell Eric to blame his parents for not being better with money.

Have you ever worried about something your parents were talking about that you didn't fully understand?

If not, think about how Eric feels, not sure what debt really means.

What does the Bible say?

"Let no debt remain outstanding, except the continuing debt to love one another." – Romans 13:8

Prayer: "Dear God, help me and my family to be wise with money and to live without the burden of debt. Help us to trust you with our needs. Amen."

Topic 78: How Can I Be Prepared Financially?

Lamont is starting to think about his future and how he can be smart with money. He knows that many adults struggle with bills and debt, and he wants to avoid that. He is in the eighth grade now, but he is already thinking about how to get scholarships to help pay for college. Lamont has been cutting grass and walking his neighbors dogs. He never brags about having money and you haven't noticed him buying any new clothes or shoes.

What would you ask Lamont?

- ☐ Lamont, how can I start learning about saving, budgeting, and making wise financial decisions early?
- ☐ Lamont, don't you think you're too young to worry about money?
- ☐ Lamont, why aren't you spending whatever money you get now and start saving later?

How do you want to handle money when you grow up?

Describe how Lamont feels, wanting to be prepared by making good choices for his future.

What does the Bible say?

"The plans of the diligent lead to profit as surely as haste leads to poverty." – Proverbs 21:5

Prayer: "Dear God, give me wisdom to manage money well and prepare for my future. Help me to learn good habits now that will bless me later. Amen."

HEALTHY HABITS

Hygiene

Shower or bathe daily.
Wear clean underwear, clothes and socks.
Clean and trim your nails.

Sleep

Go to bed early enough to allow you to feel rested when you wake up. Sleep helps you to remember what you learn and focus.

Teeth

the morning and before bed.
Scrape your tongue to reduce bacteria.
Brush your tongue.
Visit your dentist regularly.

Diet

Eat fruits and vegetables, carbs and protein. Talk to your provider about the best diet for you. Eat snacks and sweets in moderation.

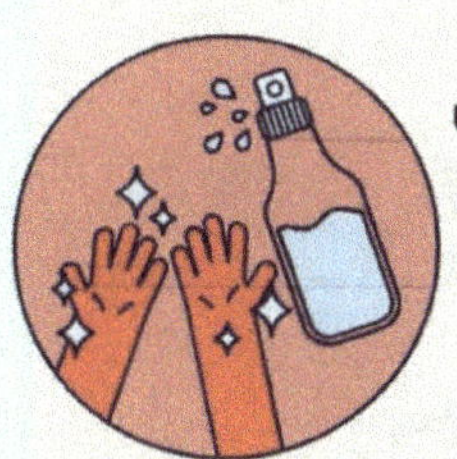

Sanitize

Use sanitizer when you are out and unable to wash your hands with soap and water, especially after touching public surfaces like door knobs, light switches, handles, bathrooms.

Homework

Complete your assignments daily. Keep your work organized. Ask questions if you don't understand. Ask for a tutor if you need one.

Topic 79: Watching Bad Videos Online

Billy's friend Marcus sits next to him on the school bus and he shows him a video online that has inappropriate content. Billy feels uncomfortable, but he's not sure if he should say anything. He knows that some of the older kids watch things like this, so he's conflicted about looking scared to watch the video. You notice that Billy looks uncomfortable and he makes eye contact with you.

What would you do?

☐ Ask Billy to come sit by you on the bus, because you have to tell him something.

☐ Tell Billy to watch it anyway so Marcus doesn't think he's boring.

☐ Tell Billy to tell Marcus that he doesn't want to watch videos like that and explain why.

Have you ever been in a situation where you felt pressured to do something that didn't feel right?

How do you think Billy feels, uncomfortable but worried about losing his friend?

What does the Bible say?

"I will not set before my eyes anything that is worthless." – Psalm 101:3

Prayer:

"Dear God, help me to choose what is good and pure to watch, and give me the courage to say no when something isn't right. Amen."

MEDIA MESSAGES VS. MEDIA EFFECTS

MEDIA MESSAGES	MEDIA EFFECTS
The values and ideas that are promoted. What is the media trying to communicate?	The influence media has on our ideas and behaviors as individuals and as a society.
Who is creating the message and how is it getting our attention?	The author/creator decides how the information will be told or framed, which can skew our views.
We interpret the message using our own experiences, views, and expectations.	Media persuades us to adopt new ideas and influences how we view the world.
The same media message can be interpreted differently, depending on the individual.	Stereotypes may be enforced and make us believe that all media reflects reality.
You should examine media messages critically. Can you find bias? Is the message conveying truth, accuracy, and fairness?	We are active users of media. We can engage with it in real time, all the time. Make choices that are productive and positive.

Topic 80: Gossiping

Heather hears some classmates talking badly about another student, Sarah, behind her back. Heather doesn't want to join in, but she also doesn't want to seem like she's taking Sarah's side. They ask your opinion about Sarah.

What would you do?

☐ Tell them that you don't have an issue with Sarah.
☐ Join in so your friends don't think you're boring.
☐ Tell them that you don't gossip, because you would say it to her face.

How do you feel about gossiping?

Describe how Heather feels, caught between wanting to do the right thing and wanting to fit in.

What does the Bible say?

"A gossip betrays a confidence, but a trustworthy person keeps a secret." – Proverbs 11:13

Prayer:

"Dear God, help me to speak kindly about others and avoid gossip. Give me the courage to stand up for what's right, even when it's hard. Amen."

Topic 81: Staying Home Alone

Jeremy has been wanting to experience staying home alone for a long time. Most of his friends get to stay home alone. Finally, his parents are going out for a date night, and they asked him if he was comfortable staying home alone, or would he prefer staying at a sitter's house. Jackson excitedly told them that he was ready to stay home alone. Jackson's parents talked to him about safety, and they reminded him to call them, or a neighbor if he gets scared. He knows not to answer the door, or go outside when they aren't home. When his parents left, it was dark outside, and he was feeling a little scared about being home alone. He tried to watch funny videos, but he kept thinking that someone could get in if they wanted to. He thought about calling his parents, but he didn't want them to take away his alone time.

What could Jeremy do?

- ☐ Lock himself in his bedroom until his parents come home.
- ☐ Call his friend and ask him to come over.
- ☐ Call his parents and tell them that he feels uncomfortable.

How can you feel safe staying at home alone?

What does the Bible say?

"The Lord himself goes before you and will be with you; he will never leave you nor forsake you. Do not be afraid; do not be discouraged." –Deuteronomy 31:8

"Dear God, please help me to be brave enough to let someone know that I am afraid. I understand that You are with me, and I understand that you also provide help for me here as well. Amen."

OUR FAMILY RULES

Be kind and honest

Respect each other's privacy

Trust in yourself

Forgive each other

Keep the house clean

Have fun together

Topic 82: The Cool Kids

Eric has always wanted to hang out with the cool kids at school, and now they've invited him to join them. However, Eric knows they often make bad decisions and treat others poorly. He's afraid if he doesn't go, he'll look lame.

What would you do?

- ☐ Encourage Eric to kindly decline and find friends who share his values.
- ☐ Tell Eric to go along with the cool kids so he can be popular, even if it means going against his values.
- ☐ Tell Eric to act like the cool kids so they'll keep inviting him to hang out.

Have you ever felt like you needed to change who you are to fit in with others? Why or why not?

Describe how Eric feels, torn between wanting to be accepted and staying true to himself.

What does the Bible say?
"You must not follow the crowd in doing wrong. When you are called to testify in a dispute, do not be swayed by the crowd to twist justice.
—Exodus 23:2

Prayer: "Dear God, help me stay true to who I am and surround myself with people who encourage me to do good. Give me the strength to say no to friends who make poor choices. Amen."

ALL ABOUT

ME

hello

MY NAME IS

I AM FROM

I AM
YEARS OLD

FAVORITE COLORS

FUN FACTS

ABOUT ME

FAVORITE FOODS

01 .

02 .

03.

WWW.CHATTERBOXTHERAPISTS.COM

Topic 83: Sneaky Crush

Kayla has a crush on her neighbor who has asked her to sneak out at night and not tell anyone. She feels torn because she likes them but knows sneaking out could get her in trouble.

What would you do?

- ☐ Encourage Kayla to tell her friend that sneaking out isn't a good idea and suggest they hang out in a safer way.
- ☐ Tell Kayla to sneak out and not tell her parents, so her friend will like her more.
- ☐ Tell Kayla to lie and say she'll sneak out but then cancel at the last minute.

Have you ever been tempted to do something risky because you had feelings for someone?

Describe how Kayla feels, liking someone but knowing that their suggestion could have serious consequences.

What does the Bible say?

"Flee the evil desires of youth and pursue righteousness, faith, love and peace." – 2 Timothy 2:22

Prayer: "Dear God, help me make wise choices, especially when I'm tempted to do something wrong because of my feelings. Keep me safe and guide me in choosing what's right. Amen."

Topic 84: A Teachable Moment

Caden's teacher asks him to stay after class to help with some assignments, but Caden feels uneasy about being alone with the teacher. He isn't sure what to do.

What would you do?

- ☐ Encourage Caden to politely say no and let another trusted adult know how he feels.
- ☐ Tell Caden to stay because it's important to do what the teacher says, even if he's uncomfortable.
- ☐ Tell Caden to make up an excuse to avoid staying without explaining his concerns.

Do you feel like you must listen to an adult, even if you feel uncomfortable? Why/Why not?

Describe how Caden feels, uncertain but wanting to make the right decision.

What does the Bible say?

"Wisdom will save you from the ways of wicked men, from men whose words are perverse." – Proverbs 2:12

Prayer:

"Dear God, give me the wisdom to recognize uncomfortable situations and the courage to speak up when something feels wrong. Help me trust adults who care about my safety. Amen."

BUILDING HEALTHY RELATIONSHIPS

AT ANY AGE

ESSENTIAL FOR BUILDING

EFFECTIVE COMMUNI-CATION

is essential for building healthy relationships, fostering understanding, resolving conflicts, and establishing trust.

SETTING BOUNDARIES

and respecting personal boundaries in relationships promotes mutual respect, emotional well-being, and healthy dynamics.

ACTIVE LISTENING SKILLS

such as paraphrasing and empathetic responses, enhancing understanding, and strengthening connections with each other.

PRACTICING SELF-LOVE AND SELF-CARE

is essential for building healthy relationships, fostering understanding, resolving conflicts, and establishing trust.

Topic 84: A Teachable Moment

Caden's teacher asks him to stay after class to help with some assignments, but Caden feels uneasy about being alone with the teacher. He isn't sure what to do.

What would you do?

- ☐ Encourage Caden to politely say no and let another trusted adult know how he feels.
- ☐ Tell Caden to stay because it's important to do what the teacher says, even if he's uncomfortable.
- ☐ Tell Caden to make up an excuse to avoid staying without explaining his concerns.

Do you feel like you must listen to an adult, even if you feel uncomfortable? Why/Why not?

Describe how Caden feels, uncertain but wanting to make the right decision.

What does the Bible say?

"Wisdom will save you from the ways of wicked men, from men whose words are perverse." – Proverbs 2:12

Prayer:

"Dear God, give me the wisdom to recognize uncomfortable situations and the courage to speak up when something feels wrong. Help me trust adults who care about my safety. Amen."

Topic 85: Positive Punishments?

Antonio got in trouble and now he is grounded for two weeks. He's not allowed to go out or use his phone, so now he's bored and frustrated.

What would you do?

- ☐ Encourage Antonio to use the time to focus on productive activities, like reading, cleaning his room, or drawing.
- ☐ Tell Antonio to sneak his phone when his parents aren't looking.
- ☐ Tell Antonio to complain and make his punishment miserable for everyone in the house.

Have you ever been grounded or put on punishment? What did you do during that time?

Describe how Antonio feels, bored but with an opportunity to use his time in a positive way.

What does the Bible say?

"No discipline seems pleasant at the time, but painful. Later on, however, it produces a harvest of righteousness and peace for those who have been trained by it." – Hebrews 12:11

Prayer:

"Dear God, help me to use my time wisely, even when I'm being disciplined. Teach me patience and responsibility and show me how to grow from this experience. Amen.

focus on
the good

Topic 86: Learning How to Prioritize

Chase has a lot of homework to do, but he also wants to play video games and watch TV. He isn't sure how to get everything done without missing out on fun.

What would you do?

☐ Encourage Chase to make a list of what's most important and focus on finishing homework first before playing.

☐ Tell Chase to ignore the homework and just have fun—he'll figure it out later.

☐ Tell Chase to rush through his homework so he can get to playing faster.

What are some ways to stay organized and prioritize your responsibilities?

Describe how Chase feels, wanting to have fun but needing to handle his responsibilities first.

What does the Bible say?

"But seek first his kingdom and his righteousness, and all these things will be given to you as well." – Matthew 6:33

Prayer:

"Dear God, help me to prioritize my responsibilities and make time for what matters most. Give me the wisdom to manage my time well. Amen."

SMART GOAL

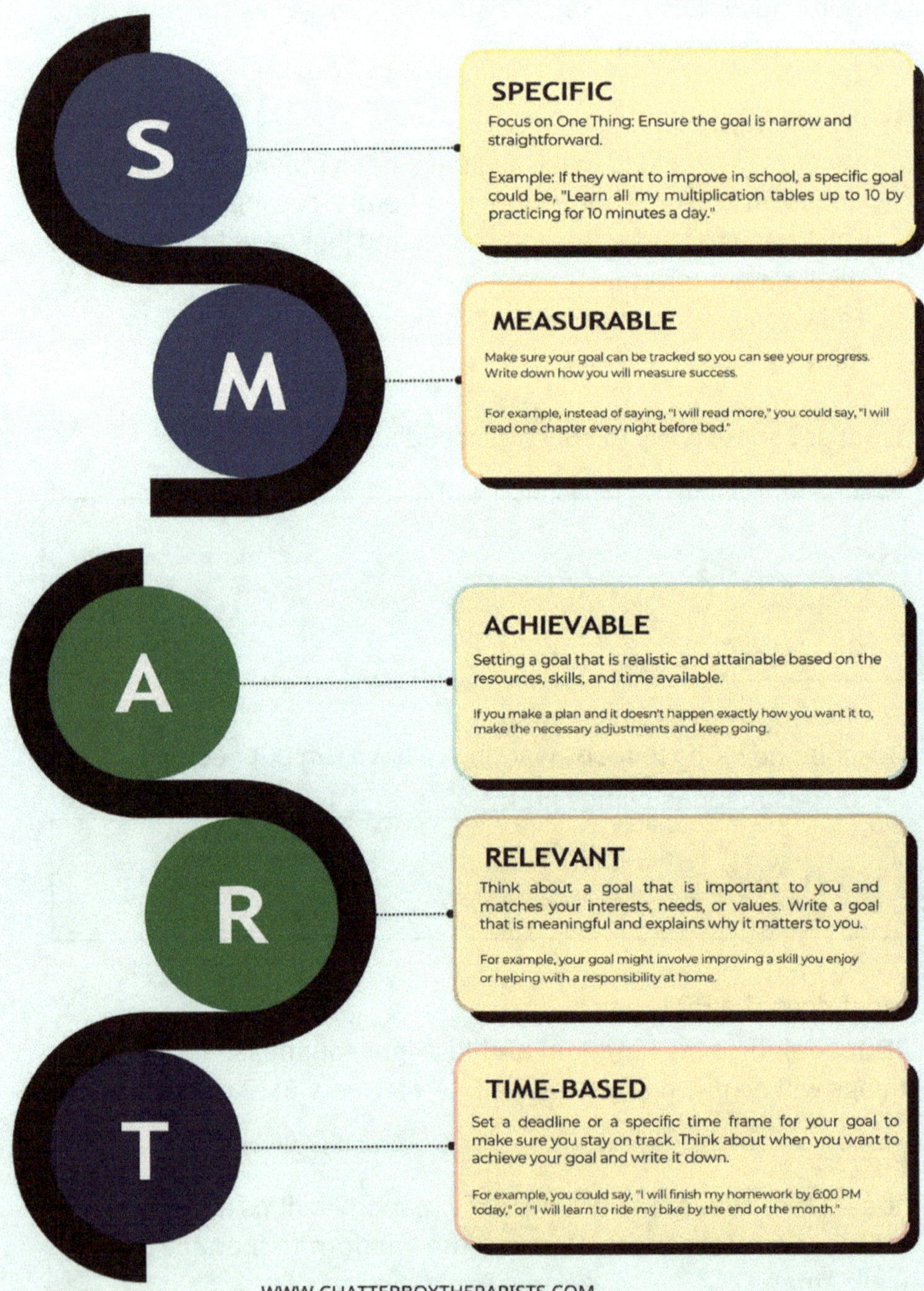
S
SPECIFIC
Focus on One Thing: Ensure the goal is narrow and straightforward.
Example: If they want to improve in school, a specific goal could be, "Learn all my multiplication tables up to 10 by practicing for 10 minutes a day."
M
MEASURABLE
Make sure your goal can be tracked so you can see your progress. Write down how you will measure success.
For example, instead of saying, "I will read more," you could say, "I will read one chapter every night before bed."
A
ACHIEVABLE
Setting a goal that is realistic and attainable based on the resources, skills, and time available.
If you make a plan and it doesn't happen exactly how you want it to, make the necessary adjustments and keep going.
R
RELEVANT
Think about a goal that is important to you and matches your interests, needs, or values. Write a goal that is meaningful and explains why it matters to you.
For example, your goal might involve improving a skill you enjoy or helping with a responsibility at home.
T
TIME-BASED
Set a deadline or a specific time frame for your goal to make sure you stay on track. Think about when you want to achieve your goal and write it down.
For example, you could say, "I will finish my homework by 6:00 PM today," or "I will learn to ride my bike by the end of the month."

MY SMARTGOAL

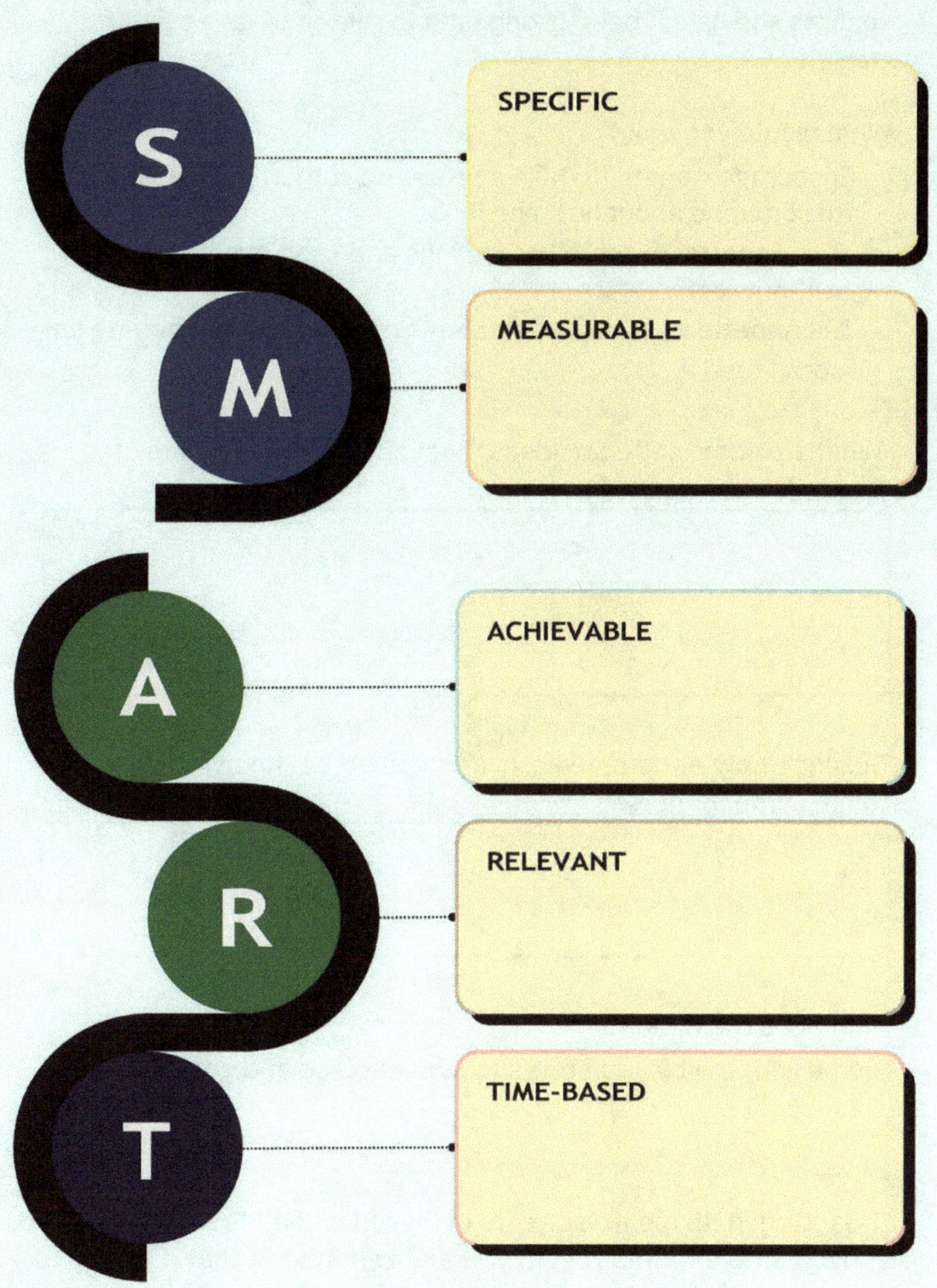

Topic 87: Self-Care

Annette feels stressed from schoolwork and friends, and she realizes she hasn't been taking time to relax and take care of herself.

What would you do?

☐ Encourage Annette to take a break, do something fun, and talk to someone about how she feels.

☐ Tell Annette to ignore her feelings and keep pushing through without rest.

☐ Tell Annette to avoid her problems by spending all her time on social media.

What are some self-care ideas that you need to take care of yourself?

Describe how Annette feels, overwhelmed but knowing she needs to take time for herself.

What does the Bible say?

"Come with me by yourselves to a quiet place and get some rest." – Mark 6:31

Prayer:

"Dear God, help me to take care of myself when I feel overwhelmed. Show me how to find rest in you and remind me that it's okay to take a break. Amen."

SelfCare

FOR A BAD DAY CHALLENGE

TRY AFFIRMATION	WALK IN NATURE
MAKE A VISION BORD	BREATHE DEEPLY
COOK YOUR FAVORITE MEAL	WRITE A JOURNAL
WATCH THE SUNRISE	GO FOR A LONG WALK
LIGHT YOUR FAVORITE CANDLE	WRITE 5 THINGS YOU LOVE
EXERCISE OR YOGA	SLEEP

WWW.CHATTERBOXTHERAPISTS.COM

Topic 88: Asking for Forgiveness

Kingston got into an argument with his friend and said some hurtful things. Now he feels bad, but doesn't know how to apologize. He has never had to ask a friend for forgiveness before, but he knows it's what he needs to do.

What would you do?

- ☐ Encourage Kingston to apologize to his friend and ask for forgiveness, even if it's hard.
- ☐ Tell Kingston to wait for his friend to apologize first, even though he knows he was wrong.
- ☐ Tell Kingston to avoid his friend until everything blows over.

What is an example of a sincere apology?

Describe how Kingston feels, knowing he needs to make things right but finding it hard to apologize.

What does the Bible say?

"Be kind and compassionate to one another, forgiving each other, just as in Christ God forgave you." – Ephesians 4:32

Prayer: "Dear God, help me to say sorry when I've hurt others. Give me the courage to ask for forgiveness and the strength to forgive those who hurt me. Amen."

Topic 89: Lying

Sade told a small lie to her mom about where she was, and now it's turning into a bigger issue. She's worried about getting caught but doesn't want to admit she lied. She's been in a similar situation before and it did not turn out well, because she had to tell a new lie to cover the old lie and it quickly got out of hand.

What would you do?

- ☐ Encourage Sade to tell the truth before things get worse.
- ☐ Tell Sade to keep lying to cover up the original lie.
- ☐ Tell Sade to blame someone else to get out of trouble.

Have you ever lied about something and then felt bad later? Describe what happened.

Describe how Sade feels, scared of getting caught but knowing she should tell the truth.

What does the Bible say?

"The Lord detests lying lips, but he delights in people who are trustworthy." – Proverbs 12:22

Prayer:

"Dear God, help me to always tell the truth, even when it's hard. Teach me the importance of honesty and guide me to be trustworthy in everything I do. Amen."

Topic 90: Good Choices and Self-Control

Marcus is at the park with his friends, and they find a can of spray paint left near the playground. One of his friends, Timmy, picks it up and suggests they use it to write their names on the park wall. Some of the other kids cheer him on, saying it's just for fun and nobody will find out. Marcus feels uncomfortable because he knows that damaging public property is wrong, but he doesn't want to look like he's being boring or scared in front of his friends.

What would you do?

- ☐ Join in and spray paint your name because you don't want to feel left out.
- ☐ Tell your friends that it's not a good idea and suggest they find something else fun to do.
- ☐ Tell your friends that you aren't going to do this and leave the park so you won't get in trouble with them if they get caught.

List examples of self-control and good choices.

What does the Bible say?

"Do not conform to the pattern of this world, but be transformed by the renewing of your mind,"

Prayer:

"Dear God, please help me make the right choices, even when others try to lead me the wrong way. Give me the courage to stand up for what's right and to be a good example to my friends. Amen."

Notes

Date:

Notes Date: ____________

Notes Date:

Notes Date:

Notes

Date: ______________

Notes

Date:

Notes

Date:

Notes

Date: ____________

Notes Date:

Notes

Date: ____________

Notes

Date: ______________

Notes

Date:

Notes

Date:

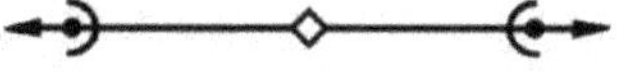

Notes Date:

Notes

Date:

Notes

Date:

Notes

Date:

Notes

Date: ____________

Notes

Date:

Notes Date: ____________

Notes

Date: ______________

Notes Date:

Notes Date: ____________

Notes

Date:

Notes

Date: ____________

Notes Date:

Notes

Date:

Notes Date: ______________

Notes

Date:

Notes Date:

Notes

Date:

Notes

Date:

Notes

Date:

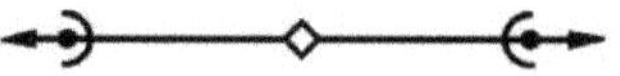

Notes Date:

Notes Date:

Notes

Date: ____________

Notes

Date:

Notes

Date:

Notes

Date:

Notes Date: